Antonia Clare   JJ Wilson

ADVANCED

Total English
Workbook (with key)

PEARSON
Longman

Contents

1 Challenges

LESSON 1.1 (p4–5)
Reading: Feeling on top of the world
Grammar: prepositions
Vocabulary: phrases about language
Listening: polyglots

LESSON 1.2 (p6–7)
Vocabulary: talking about how much you know
Grammar: passives
Listening: news stories
Pronunciation: word stress

LESSON 1.3 (p8–9)
Reading: Nerves of steel
Vocabulary: achievement
Grammar: perfect aspect
How to: talk about an achievement
Writing: a paragraph about achievement

Review and consolidation unit 1 (p10–11)

2 Community

LESSON 2.1 (p12–13)
Listening: embarrassing moments abroad
Grammar: verb patterns
How to: give advice/make recommendations about places
Vocabulary: being polite

LESSON 2.2 (p14–15)
Grammar: comparatives
How to: recognise informal writing
Reading: Internet millionaires

LESSON 2.3 (p16–17)
Listening: community living
Vocabulary: describing places

Review and consolidation unit 2 (p18–19)

3 Tales

LESSON 3.1 (p20–21)
Reading: The old age hoax
Grammar: narrative tenses
Pronunciation: differentiating similar sounds and words

LESSON 3.2 (p22–23)
Reading and listening: Birdwatcher
Vocabulary: describing books
How to: describe people
Vocabulary: compound adjectives

LESSON 3.3 (p24–25)
Listening: jokes
Grammar: participles/gerunds
Vocabulary: types of humour

Review and consolidation unit 3 (p26–27)

4 Progress

LESSON 4.1 (p28–29)
Vocabulary: progress
Reading: superheroes
Grammar: future probability/possibility/certainty
Listening: Real-life superheroes

LESSON 4.2 (p30–31)
Vocabulary: talking about plans/free time
Grammar: future tenses review
Reading: 'Slow movement' encourages less stressful living
How to: sound vague

LESSON 4.3 (p32–33)
Vocabulary: special abilities
Reading: Nine-year-old calls the shots
Grammar: inversion

Review and consolidation unit 4 (p34–35)

5 Fortunes

LESSON 5.1 (p36–37)
Vocabulary: finance
Grammar: emphasis
Reading and listening: Child of the incarcerated

LESSON 5.2 (p38–39)
Vocabulary: colloquial phrases
Grammar: conditionals
Vocabulary: charity
Reading: Instant millionaires need help

LESSON 5.3 (p40–41)
Vocabulary: in the office
How to: express priorities
Grammar: sentence adverbials
Listening: MediaCom
Vocabulary: express quantity

Review and consolidation unit 5 (p42–43)

6 Power

LESSON 6.1 (p44–45)
Listening: new wonders of the world
Pronunciation: speed and rhythm in connected speech
Grammar: articles
How to: describe an important building/structure
Writing: an essay

LESSON 6.2 (p46–47)
Reading: Student power
Grammar: *whatever/whoever/whenever/however*
Vocabulary: phrasal verbs

LESSON 6.3 (p48–49)
Listening: charisma
Grammar: link words of time and contrast
Vocabulary: describing people

Review and consolidation unit 6 (p50–51)

7 Nature

LESSON 7.1 (p52–53)
Reading: The dog with the golden nose
Grammar: relative clauses
Vocabulary: collocations
How to: explain procedures

LESSON 7.2 (p54–55)
Reading and listening: Nature's extremes
Grammar: verb patterns
Vocabulary: description

LESSON 7.3 (p56–57)
Grammar: *as ... as*, describing quantity
Pronunciation: *as* (weak form)
Vocabulary: buying and selling
Writing: an advertisement
Listening: working with animals

Review and consolidation unit 7 (p58–59)

8 Issues

LESSON 8.1 (p60–61)
Listening: Future world
Vocabulary: giving opinions
Grammar: reporting verbs
How to: stall for time

LESSON 8.2 (p62–63)
Grammar: continuous and simple
Vocabulary: lifestyles
Reading: Twenty ways to beat stress

LESSON 8.3 (p64–65)
Listening: phone messages
Grammar: fronting
Vocabulary: cause and effect
How to: describe everyday problems
Writing: linking and sequencing expressions

Review and consolidation unit 8 (p66–67)

9 Vision

LESSON 9.1 (p68–69)
Vocabulary: the arts
Grammar: dependent prepositions
How to: express certainty and uncertainty
Reading: Stephen Hawking

LESSON 9.2 (p70–71)
Vocabulary: describing art
How to: say what you like/dislike
Grammar: discourse markers
Vocabulary: crime
Reading: art forgeries

LESSON 9.3 (p72–73)
Vocabulary: cameras and photos
Grammar: unreal past
How to: respond to hypothetical questions
Listening: interview with a photographer

Review and consolidation unit 9 (p74–75)

10 Feelings

LESSON 10.1 (p76–77)
Listening and vocabulary: feelings
Grammar: modals
Vocabulary: idioms

LESSON 10.2 (p78–79)
Grammar: modals of deduction
Vocabulary: strong adjectives of feeling
Reading: What I've learned about husbands

LESSON 10.3 (p80–81)
Reading: Paddy Clarke Ha, Ha, Ha
Grammar: uses of *would*
How to: describe a childhood memory
Listening: a childhood memory

Review and consolidation unit 10 (p82–83)

Answer key (p84–95)

1.1 Challenges

Reading

1 Read the text. Mark the statements true (T) or false (F)?

1 Mark Inglis had both his legs amputated after a climbing accident in 1982. ☐
2 He never found the courage to return to climb the mountain where the accident happened. ☐
3 On reaching the top of Everest, Mark found he was hardly able to speak. ☐
4 Sir Edmund Hillary and the Prime Minister of New Zealand were among the people to congratulate Mark on his achievement. ☐
5 Mark broke one of his artificial legs when climbing down the mountain. ☐
6 Mark had taken several replacement legs with him on the climb. ☐
7 Mark's main problem during the climb was that he needed to go very slowly. ☐
8 Before his legs were amputated Mark had also won a silver medal for cycling in the Olympics. ☐
9 Helen Clark, who doesn't climb herself, feels that Mark is setting a good example to people with disabilities. ☐

2 a Complete the questions using words from the box.

> make   daunting   set   ambition
> without   face   rising   attitude

1 How did Mark _____ achievable goals?
2 What challenges did he _____?
3 Did Mark succeed in _____ to the challenge?
4 How did he _____ his dream come true?
5 What couldn't Mark have done it _____?
6 What advice does Miss Clark give to people with a burning _____?
7 Do you think Mark had the right _____?
8 What would you consider most _____ about his challenge?

b Answer the questions.

Feeling on top of the world

The first man with no legs to climb to the top of Mount Everest was almost speechless when he reached the summit and called his wife by satellite phone.

Mark Inglis, forty-seven, who lost both legs in a climbing accident twenty-four years ago, was suffering an attack of laryngitis and managed only to croak: 'I did it!'

Sir Edmund Hillary, eighty-six, who conquered the world's highest peak in May 1953, was among the first to offer his congratulations. 'It's a remarkable effort. He's done a pretty good job,' he said.

According to members of his party, his short conversation with his wife Anne when he spoke from the summit were among the few words he was able to utter.

Asked by New Zealand television how the climb had been, he managed to say only: 'Bloody hard.'

His wife said one of his carbon fibre artificial legs snapped on the ascent, but was quickly replaced from a bundle of spare legs and parts taken with him.

Wayne Alexander, one of three climbing companions up the 29,035 feet summit, said: 'What Mark did was absolutely remarkable. I have never seen such human endurance.' Speaking from Advance Base Camp on the mountain, he added: 'He did so well. It was a bit like chasing a greyhound – he was gone.'

Helen Clark, the New Zealand Prime Minister, said: 'To reach the summit of Everest is a once-in-a-lifetime achievement, but for Mark Inglis it will be even more satisfying. He has said it was a childhood dream to stand on the roof of the world, but he thought he had lost it when he lost his legs.'

He had his legs amputated below the knees due to frostbite, suffered in 1982 while he was trapped for fourteen days by blizzards on Mount Cook, the highest peak in New Zealand.

He went on to become the first double amputee to reach the mountain's summit, and followed this achievement by conquering 26,906 feet Mount Cho Oyu in Tibet, the world's sixth highest peak. He also won a silver medal for cycling in the 2000 Sydney Paralympic Games.

Miss Clark, a keen amateur climber, added that Mr Inglis had sent a signal to others with disabilities 'that your ambitions should never be limited'.

Grammar | prepositions

3 Choose the correct alternative.

1 We finally opted *to/for/on* the silver colour.
2 It is a method of distinguishing cancer cells *from/between/of* normal tissue.
3 Very few people succeed *on losing/to lose/in losing* weight and keeping it off!
4 His headaches stemmed *from/with/to* vision problems.
5 It is most likely to appeal *at/to/with* the younger generation.
6 I wouldn't bother *in/to/about* calling him now.
7 We all came to rely *on/in/with* her judgement.
8 We want him to get the maximum benefit *of/from/with* the course.
9 Can you lend me a few dollars? I'm a bit short *on/of/with* money at the moment.
10 The wall of the prison was riddled *of/in/with* bullet holes.
11 She seems to be lacking *with/on/in* confidence.
12 They weren't at all nervous *about/with/for* asking for a rise.

Vocabulary | phrases about language

4 Complete the mini-dialogues using the words in the box.

> delight   slide   ball   overload
> garbled   cramming   picked   master

1 A: How is your German nowadays?
   B: It's terrible. I've really let it _____ .
2 A: I didn't know you could speak Thai!
   B: I can't really. I just _____ up a few words while I was there on holiday.
3 A: How long did it take you to _____ the grammar?
   B: Years! I used to spend a lot of time _____ information from grammar books until I had complete information _____ .
4 A: Have you heard from Simon?
   B: He left a _____ message which I can't understand.
5 A: What do you enjoy most about being able to speak Russian?
   B: The sheer _____ of being able to talk to people I meet there.
6 A: I can't believe how quickly she's learnt the language.
   B: Yes, she's very on the _____ .

Listening

5 🔊 1.1 Cover the tapescript. Listen to an extract from a radio programme. Answer the questions.

1 What is different about a polyglot's brain?
2 What do scientists hope to achieve through doing the new research?
3 What did people have to distinguish between during the trial?
4 How did the researchers decide who was a 'good' language learner?
5 What is the function of fibres in the brain's white matter?
6 What can you tell from the brain scans?

> **TAPESCRIPT**
>
> Polyglots 'have different brains'. New research has shown that people with a gift for other languages could actually have different types of brains from other people. Neuroscientists at University College London say that polyglots have more 'white brain matter' in a part of the brain which processes sound. It is hoped that the research published in a medical journal could be used to help identify reasons for language difficulties.
>
> During a trial involving native French speakers, people were asked to distinguish between two similar sounds from different languages. The first was the 'd' sound found in French. The second was a 'd' found in Hindi, which is pronounced in a different way. Researchers tested the speed at which participants could process the information about the different sounds. People who were successful on this task were asked to listen to other similar sounds.
>
> Some of the fastest learners were able to tell the sounds apart within a few minutes, while the slowest learners were only able to make random guesses after twenty minutes of training.
>
> Dr Narly Golestani from UCL's Institute of Cognitive Neuroscience said the brain's white matter was involved in the efficient processing of sound information. Its fibres are involved in connecting brain regions together. Fast language learners had a greater volume of white matter, and that may mean they have more or perhaps thicker fibres.
>
> 'We are starting to understand that brain shape and structure can be informative about people's abilities – why people are good at some things and not others is evident from these scans,' she said.
>
> White brain matter is involved in connecting different parts of the brain together, and greater amounts of this could indicate an increased ability to process sound. Previous research suggested that having a talent for music was linked to the structure of grey matter in the brain.
>
> 'This latest research could be used in other ways,' Dr Narly said. 'We can start to make predictions regarding whether people will be good at something or not based on their brain structure or even to diagnose clinical problems.'

1.2

Vocabulary | talking about how much you know

1 Match the sentences halves.

1 We had to learn poems by ☐
2 I grew up here. I know it like the back ☐
3 I know next to ☐
4 She knew without a ☐
5 Just off the top of my ☐
6 I'm pretty ☐
7 As far as the Americans ☐
8 Have you ever heard of ☐
9 Erikson knew the game ☐
10 Do you know offhand ☐

a doubt that this was where she wanted to be.
b head I'd say there were about fifty.
c are concerned, a lot of our hotels are below standard.
d of my hand.
e David Marshall?
f heart when I was at school.
g what time the show starts?
h sure he'll say yes.
i nothing about antiques.
j inside out.

Reading and Grammar | passives

2 Read the article. <u>Underline</u> examples of the passives used for distancing and other distancing structures.

Notable lasts

1
Lillian Asplund, who died aged ninety-nine, was the last American survivor of the Titanic, and the only living person with any memory of the events of 15 April 1912. She was five years old when the ship went down in the freezing waters of the north Atlantic, taking with it her father and three of her brothers. As she was winched to safety in a lifeboat, she saw them peering at her over the ship's railing. The image is said to have haunted her for the rest of her life, and despite the world's ongoing fascination with the Titanic, it seems she rarely spoke of the tragedy.

2
Martha is thought to have been the last surviving carrier pigeon. Carrier pigeons were probably once the most common bird in the world. It is estimated that there were as many as five billion carrier pigeons in the United States. They lived in enormous flocks, sometimes up to a mile wide and 300 miles long, taking several days to pass and probably containing two billion birds. They were hunted to extinction by humans. Martha, the last of her species, died in Cincinnati Zoo, in 1914. She was then frozen in a block of ice and her body was sent to The Smithsonian Institution, where she can still be seen.

3
Ishi was the name given to the last member of the Yahi tribe of California, and means 'man' in the Yahi language. Ishi is believed to be the last native American in Northern California to have lived the bulk of his life completely outside the European American culture. He was thought to have left his homeland in the foothills near Lassen Peak, California, and was found when he emerged from the wild on 29th August 1911. His real name was never known, because in his society it was taboo to say one's own name. Since he was the last member of his tribe, his real name died with him.

3 Complete the sentences using words or phrases from the text.
1 Two men were _____ out of the sinking boat by an RAF helicopter. (para 1)
2 Jimmy was _____ through the wet windscreen at the cars ahead. (para 1)
3 Clare was _____ by the fear that her husband was having an affair. (para 1)
4 Police knew of his _____ with guns. (para 1)
5 We glanced up in surprise as a _____ of wild geese flew noisily overhead. (para 2)
6 The nearest hotel might be _____ away. (para 2)
7 This rare breed was on the verge of _____ . (para 2)
8 The _____ of our clients are young professionals. (para 3)
9 We went skiing in the _____ of the Alps. (para 3)
10 There were cheers as the sun _____ from behind the clouds. (para 3)

4 Complete the texts using the passive for distancing. Use the verbs in brackets. Add extra words if necessary.

It (1) _____ (say) Thomas Edison, the famous inventor, believed that taking off one's clothing caused insomnia. It (2) _____ (seem) he often slept in his clothes on newspapers beneath the stairs in his laboratory.

Alexander Graham Bell, inventor of the telephone, (3) _____ (claim) to have first answered the device by saying 'hoy, hoy' instead of 'hello'!

Joseph Gayetty invented toilet paper in 1857, and (4) _____ (think) to have had his name printed on each sheet.

Charles Goodyear, who (5) _____ (say) to have been instrumental in establishing the rubber industry in the US, (6) _____ (think) to have carried out his first experiments in jail. It (7) _____ (seem) though he had been imprisoned for failure to pay his debts.

Leonardo da Vinci (8) _____ (think) to have designed a military tank in the fifteenth century. Remarkably, he (9) _____ (believe) to have also worked on designs for hot-air balloons and deep-sea diving suits.

Joseph Merlin, a Belgian musician, invented roller skates in 1760. He (10) _____ (appear) to have first demonstrated them at a ball by skating across the room playing a violin.

Listening

5 **1.2** Cover the tapescript. Listen to the news stories. Do the tasks below.
1 Write down the key words.
2 Listen again.
3 Write down the story exactly as you hear it.
4 Check with the tapescript.

Pronunciation | word stress

6 a Listen and read aloud at the same time. Which words carry the main stress? Are these the key words you chose in Ex. 5?

b Practise reading aloud at the same time as listening. Try to imitate the rhythm of the speaker.

TAPESCRIPT

Foreign visitors to Naples are to be given cheap plastic watches as part of an attempt to combat the street crime for which the city has become notorious. Drug dealing, auto theft and street muggings are increasingly common crime trends, creating problems for visitors and residents alike.

Moscow has been named the most expensive city in the world. Mercer, the human resources consultants, have compared costs internationally of 200 items and concluded that the cost of living in the Russian capital is twelve percent higher than in London. Price rises in Moscow have been fuelled by a recent property boom.

More than eighty people were killed during gang violence in the state of São Paolo over the weekend in a wave of attacks on prisons and police stations. Most of the victims were police officers and prison guards, murdered in apparent retaliation for a criminal crackdown that began last month.

Hundreds of thousands of Spaniards have been demanding help from the government after losing their savings in a pyramid selling scam involving rare stamps. The 'Enron of Spain', as it has been labelled by experts, is the biggest financial scam that the country has ever known, and may have grave repercussions on the Spanish economy.

1.3

Reading

1 **a** Read the interview. Answer the questions.

1 What kinds of races does Annie compete in?
2 What is her ambition?
3 How did her parents influence her?
4 What injuries has she suffered?
5 How does she cope when she is hurt?

b Find words or expressions in the text which mean:

1 long for/strongly desire (para 1) _____
2 do on your own (para 1) _____
3 only just (para 1) _____
4 satisfy her desire for doing well (para 2) _____
5 something she really wants to achieve (para 2) _____
6 be an equally strong competitor (para 2) _____
7 inspired/impressed (para 3) _____
8 be very keen to do something (para 4) _____
9 be able to do (para 4) _____
10 give up (para 5) _____
11 self-determination (para 5) _____
12 continued despite difficulties (para 5) _____

c Complete the sentences. Use the correct form of the words and phrases from Ex. 1b.

1 He is extremely ambitious. His _____ is to take over the whole company.
2 Ellen MacArthur sailed _____ around the world.
3 My job is getting so stressful, I'm thinking about _____ .
4 They had _____ left the office when the police arrived.
5 The New Zealand team are very fit, and will prove to be a _____ for the Irish.
6 I was _____ adventure, so I signed up for a trip across Africa.
7 I'm not sure that they're entirely _____ finishing the job.

Nerves of steel

1 She's blonde, charming, enthusiastic and above all extremely determined. If you only judge Annie Seel by her looks, you're in for the greatest of surprises. There are other women motorcyclists for sure, but how many crave extreme adventure in such a way, and how many take on single-handedly all the toughest rallies the world has to offer? Addicted early on to speed and adrenaline, the desert princess switched from horse to motorcycle races when she was barely sixteen.

2 Twenty years and seventeen broken bones on, she continues to try to quench her thirst for success and for new records to break, as much at home up Mount Everest as on African rallies, on tarmac races as on Mexican bajas. Can you guess the ultimate quest for this woman of one metre fifty-five? To be a true match for her male colleagues in the greatest races, starting with this Rallye Maroc in which she's riding in the marathon class.

3 Annie, what gave you this taste for extreme adventure?
'I grew up next to a racecourse. I quickly got addicted to speed, and then at sixteen I saw some motorcycle stuntmen at a show. I was awed. I bought myself a motorcycle, but none of my friends liked speed the same as me. Then when I was eighteen I started to do road racing and finished eighth in the Swedish Championships ...'

4 And in 2000 you tried a rally in Dubai ...
'I went to Morocco and fell in love with the desert. I was desperate to do a race. I ordered a DIY Husaberg 600 and assembled it barely ten days before the start.
I rode on my own and made straight for the sand dunes. On the last day I got a fractured foot but I still got to the finish in forty-ninth place. Since then I've been to Tunisia and Argentina. This Moroccan race is my sixth one in the World Championships. I'm trying to show what I'm capable of doing with the hope of finding some money for the Dakar in 2006. To tell you the truth, it's fairly hard to find any in Sweden for these kinds of races ... '

5 What's most impressive about you is your determination. You've broken your bones seventeen times, yet you've never given up.
'No, I never quit. My father, who died when I was sixteen, gave me a taste for mechanical things, and my mother gave me fairly exceptionally strong will power. When I broke my hand on the fourth stage of the Dakar in 2002, I held on till the end. My left leg had gone blue all over. I'll admit, though, that I've always been lucky enough to have injuries that didn't prevent me from finishing the race. When I run into a problem, I shriek a bit and then I carry on.'

Vocabulary | achievement

2 Complete the sentences using words from the box.

> born greatest persevered
> pushing faces pursue heading
> deal triumphs constraints begged

1 She _____ and pleaded with them until they finally agreed.
2 You need to keep your priorities in order if you want to _____ your dream.
3 _____ on spending have forced the company to rethink its plans.
4 The President _____ the difficult task of putting the economy back on its feet.
5 My tutor was always _____ me to do better.
6 Winning the championship is one of our _____ _____ .
7 He was _____ to be a politician.
8 We have had to _____ with a lot of unnecessary criticism.
9 She _____ in her claim for insurance, and in the end it paid off.
10 I'm afraid they may be _____ for trouble.

Grammar | perfect aspect

3 Complete the text using the correct form of the verbs in brackets.

Round-the-world cyclist Heinz Stucke has an aura of calm about him. By the end of this year he (1) _____ (be) on the road for over forty-four years. The German cyclist, who (2) _____ (travel) a third of a million miles, through 211 territories, arrived in Portsmouth last week. Within hours of getting off the ferry from France, the bicycle that (3) _____ (be) his constant companion since 1962 was stolen. But he's not bitter.

'I trust everybody,' he said, 'because if you didn't, you just wouldn't go around the world. You take a calculated risk everywhere you go.'

In fact, his bike – a unique artefact which (4) _____ already _____ (be requested) by a museum of cycling back in Germany – was returned to him little more than thirty-six hours after its theft. Heinz was expecting it. Before this, the bike (5) _____ already _____ (be) stolen on five previous occasions. 'The last time (6) _____ (be) in 1997 – almost every ten years it has been stolen. That's not bad in 150,000 kilometres.'

This is not the only problem Heinz (7) _____ (have) to deal with. Since 1962 – when he (8) _____ (give up) his job as a toolmaker in a small town in Germany and (9) _____ (set off) on his odyssey – Stucke (10) _____ (be attacked) twice by swarms of bees, and (11) _____ (shoot) in the foot by Zambian guerrillas. He (12) _____ often _____ (be) hungry (he makes a living by selling a book about his experiences) and exhausted: at one point, his bicycle (13) _____ (rust) because of the sweat dripping off his nose. And then there's the loneliness. 'I (14) _____ (have) many little affairs,' he says. 'But now it's more complicated: I'm sixty-six and on a bicycle, and I sleep in a tent ...'

How to ... | talk about an achievement

4 Complete the text with the extracts A–I.

A I really feel I have accomplished something
B I'd never been involved in catering before
C exactly the kind of environment I wanted to achieve.
D maybe in a couple of year's time
E One of my greatest achievements
F opened Café Mundo six months ago
G and I've had to learn a lot very quickly
H so we decided to buy it
I I'd always dreamed of

(1) _____ is finally to have set up my own business with a friend. (2) _____ running a small café, with a bookshop inside. I wanted it to be a place where people can come to enjoy a coffee, read a book, listen to music, or chat to friends. I had a very clear vision in my head of (3) _____ . Last year, I found the perfect location for the café (4) _____ . It was a big gamble as (5) _____ , but we spent a few months renovating the building and (6) _____ . It's been an incredibly hard year, (7) _____ , but it's been a great experience and (8) _____ . We're thinking of opening a second café, (9) _____ .

Writing

5 Use the model in Ex. 4 to write a paragraph about a personal achievement, or about an achievement which you particularly admire.

9

Review and consolidation unit 1

Passives

1 Choose the correct word or phrase to complete the sentences.

1 It is widely _____ eating too many fatty foods causes heart disease.
  A believing   B to be believed of   C believed that
  D believed to be

2 The notes from last month's meeting _____ lost.
  A are appeared   B seem to have be
  C appear that they are   D seem to have been

3 It seems _____ Mr Klein was wrong about the figures.
  A as though   B if   C as to   D as

4 Is the shipment _____ this afternoon?
  A be delivered   B being delivered   C deliver
  D to deliver

5 Smoking _____ allowed on planes for years.
  A isn't being   B isn't   C hasn't been   D doesn't

6 The governing body decided that the postponed game _____ next week.
  A must be played   B must have been played
  C will play   D will be being played

7 It _____ by various journalists that the scandal was caused by government corruption.
  A is being asserted   B has being said
  C was suggest   D did assert

8 _____ in the past that the world was flat?
  A Was there assumed   B Did it assume
  C Was assumed   D Was it assumed

9 Reuben _____ the most handsome man in London society.
  A has said to be   B was said to be   C was to be
  D was said

10 The company _____ gone bankrupt because of increased competition.
  A is thought   B is said to be   C said to have
  D is thought to have

2 Match the sentence halves.

1 She is said to ☐
2 It was widely ☐
3 The robbers were thought ☐
4 Judging by this map, we appear to have ☐
5 It seems as though ☐
6 You look as ☐
7 The competition entry must ☐
8 The wedding cake will have been ☐

a made by now.
b if you've just seen a ghost.
c to have escaped.
d be a genius.
e be submitted tomorrow.
f the weather will get better.
g got completely lost.
h assumed that Dobson would inherit his father's money.

Perfect aspect

3 Complete the sentences using the perfect aspect.

1 By this time next week we _____ school and I'll be on holiday!
2 It was only when Mariana told me her name that I _____ met before.
3 The children were all sunburned. They _____ football in the sun all day.
4 She looks exhausted because she _____ well recently. She needs a new bed.
5 Even by next July Kazunari probably _____ writing his thesis.
6 Oh no! _____ the key in the car and it's locked!
7 Yesterday, Mr Jones finally received his visa. He _____ to get one for years.
8 Wow! Fantastic news! I _____ a scholarship by the university.
9 We went to a Mowgli concert. I _____ of them before, but they were very good.
10 By tomorrow, Don _____ here for over fifty years! He started as an office boy.

4 Is the sentence in *italics* replying to statement A or B?

1 A We haven't been feeding the cat enough food.
  B We haven't fed the cat enough food.
  I know. He's started catching mice again recently. ☐

2 A How many countries will you have visited after this trip?
  B How many countries will you visit on this trip?
  Eighteen if you include the one where I was born! ☐

3 A We haven't been told the itinerary.
  B We hadn't been told the itinerary.
  Well, I think the conference starts at 9.00 and you're speaking at 11.00. ☐

4 A I've been sitting quietly, minding my own business.
  B I'd been sitting quietly, minding my own business.
  And then what happened? ☐

5 A Where have you put the money?
  B Where will you have put the money?
  I put it where you told me to. ☐

6 A I'd always wanted a place of my own.
  B I've always wanted a place of my own.
  Well, congratulations! It's a really nice house. ☐

Prepositional phrases

5 Complete the article with the correct form of words from the box plus a preposition.

> opt succeed reminiscent short appeal
> bother nervous subject rely benefit

Holiday challenge

Holiday Challenge is guaranteed to (1) _____ _____ your adventurous spirit. We provide a choice of parachute jumps, hang gliding, rock climbing and kayaking. You can (2) _____ _____ two sports plus board and luxury lodging for just $300 a week! If you're (3) _____ _____ cash, you can choose the economy camping option at $175.

What if you are (4) _____ _____ trying a new sport? Don't worry. You can (5) _____ _____ us to provide the best training available to ensure that you're safe. And we won't (6) _____ you _____ any 5.00 a.m. starts or boot camp horrors! Read what our customers have said about us.

'I really (7) _____ _____ my two weeks with Holiday Challenge. It was an amazing experience!' (Cal Jones, New York)

'It was (8) _____ _____ my childhood: running around, learning new stuff, without a care in the world. The best holiday I've ever had.' (Jill Healey, UK)

'Don't (9) _____ _____ checking the competitors. Holiday Challenge is the one.' (Sanath Kuppara, Sri Lanka)

'I (10) _____ _____ living my dreams! Thank you, Holiday Challenge.' (Macarena Duval, Chile)

Vocabulary

6 Complete the sentences by adding or cutting one word.
1. Paulo Freire? Who's he? I've never heard him.
2. The Whorf-Sapir hypothesis? I know it like in the back of my hand.
3. Wendy's phone number? I don't know it by offhand.
4. Shakespeare's love poems? We spent years learning them by the heart.
5. Is Ronaldinho the best footballer in the world? Without but a doubt.
6. The Highway Code? Ask Susie – she's a driving instructor. She knows it inside.
7. International banking? I know next nothing about it.
8. Was Matisse the greatest painter in history? As far as I'm, he was.

7 a Add a prefix to the words in *italics* to make the sentences correct.
1. She couldn't finish the race because she's totally ___*fit*.
2. I read an article recently about ___*paid* bosses who earn millions for doing virtually nothing.
3. I just couldn't do any work because I was feeling so ___*motivated*.
4. Only a fool would ___*estimate* Thomson; she has the potential to be a great leader.
5. The workers are all ___*-smokers* so no one has ever asked for a smoking area.
6. He's a ___*-professional* footballer. He does it part-time for about £100 a week.
7. The problem was that they had ___*understood* the instructions, which is why the mistake occurred.
8. I'm totally ___*worked*. I have to organise a conference and write seven reports in two days.
9. Your excuses are completely ___*relevant* to me! You should have done your homework on time!
10. Davies was ___*aware* of the plan to fire him, which is why it was such a shock when it happened.

b Number the lines 1–11 in the correct order.

[1] Climber Rheinhold Messner always knew that he had the

[ ] challenge. Most doctors and scientists suggested that this was not an achievable

[ ] come true with a successful three-day ascent.

[ ] all expectations. After a few months' preparation, Messner pursued his dream

[ ] something truly amazing in the mountains. However, in 1980 he exceeded

[ ] of risk about climbing Everest, but Messner's attempt to take

[ ] of being the first man to ascend Everest without oxygen supplies. There is always an element

[ ] potential to accomplish

[ ] on the world's highest mountain with the

[ ] goal. Against all expectations, on 20th August he made his dream

[ ] constraint of no oxygen was a truly daunting

2.1 Community

Listening

1 a ▶ 2.1 Cover the tapescript. Listen to three speakers describing embarrassing moments abroad. Complete the table.

	Speaker 1	Speaker 2	Speaker 3
Nationality of speaker	(1) _____	(5) _____	(9) _____
Country where embarrassing moment happened	(2) _____	(6) _____	(10) _____
Main problem	(3) _____	(7) _____	(11) _____
Speaker's final thoughts about the situation	(4) _____	(8) _____	(12) _____

TAPESCRIPT

1

After a ten-hour journey from London I was really happy to have arrived at my host family's house in Colombia. They were extremely friendly even though I spoke only a little Spanish, and they plied me with lemonade and made me feel comfortable. After a while, the mother asked me: 'Estas casado'? I thought she was asking me if I was tired, so I said: 'Si, un poco,' which means 'yes, a little'. Suddenly everyone laughed. Later I found out that 'casado' means married, and 'cansado' means tired. So she'd asked me if I was married and I'd said: 'Oh, a little'! That was just the first of many linguistic blunders I made! Actually, looking back, I wish I'd learned more of the language before moving there, but at the time I thought I'd just muddle through. Bad idea.

2

I'm from Colombia but I've lived in the US for ten years. When I first got a car, I needed to buy gas so I drove to a gas station and sat there waiting to be served. And I sat there, and I sat there, and no one came. Eventually, a bit perplexed, I went into the store and asked for a full tank of gas. The girl took my money, and I went back to the car and waited again. Still no one came. So I thought maybe someone had done it for me while I was in the store. So I drove off. But then I looked at the gasometer and the tank was completely empty. I drove back to the gas station and suddenly I realised I had to fill the car myself. I've never done this before because in Colombia the people who work at the gas station do it for you. Well, I felt a bit stupid, as you can imagine.

3

This was before I could speak English properly. I was flying back to Italy and I was at Heathrow. Now, for some reason or other, I didn't have my glasses and I'm very short sighted so I couldn't see the information on the screen. So I asked someone official-looking: 'Which gate for Milan?' and he said: 'It's too early. There's no gate.' Now I got a bit confused because I thought that 'early' meant 'late', so I began to panic, thinking I'd missed my flight. So I asked someone else, and again: 'You're too early. No gate assigned. You'll have to wait.' And I was tearing my hair out and wondering why these English people were so calm when I'd just missed my flight. Eventually, a nice Englishman explained, very pleasantly, that the gate number would appear very soon and that I hadn't missed my flight. He was probably thinking: 'Dumb tourist.' So the moral of the story is: learn the basics. And don't lose your glasses!

b Listen again and check.

c Now read the tapescript. Find words or phrases which mean:
1 give someone large amounts of food or drink (speaker 1) _____
2 stupid mistakes (speaker 1) _____
3 continue doing something even though you aren't very good at it (speaker 1) _____
4 confused by something (speaker 2) _____
5 formal word for *given*, e.g. a task or a seat (speaker 3) _____
6 idiom for going crazy/getting angry (speaker 3) _____

2.1

Grammar | verb patterns

2 Choose the correct alternative.
1. The Agency advises tourists *to take/taking/take* traveller's cheques rather than cash.
2. We look forward to *meet/meeting/have met* you in June.
3. My parents always encouraged me *that/write/writing/to write* down my thoughts.
4. After graduating, Louise thought *of travel/of travelling/to travel* for a year, but decided against it.
5. Mark recommended *ride/her to ride/riding* a bicycle as a good way to get fit.
6. They couldn't afford *to waste/that they waste/wasting* time on trivial matters.
7. I would urge *to reconsider/you to reconsider/you reconsider* the offer before it's too late.
8. We've avoided *to do/that we do/doing* anything too dangerous so far.
9. I object *I have to/to having to/I have to* pay for my own travel to these conferences.
10. Chiara persuaded *us that we go/us go/us to go* on a boat trip with her.

3 Complete the text using the correct form of verbs from the box. Add extra words where necessary.

> change   hear   make   find out   object
> take   live   advise   think   afford

Culture shock

Those people thinking (1) _____ abroad will face a number of challenges including communication difficulties and settling in to a new community. But perhaps the biggest challenge is culture shock. You may find yourself (2) _____ to everything about the host culture; the way the people drive, queue, greet you, their habits and attitudes towards everything around you such as litter and personal space. This is common. People cannot avoid (3) _____ that their own culture does things 'the right way'. Everything else is therefore wrong. We urge you (4) _____ your mindset. There are no cultural rights or wrongs, only differences. What's more, if you're committed to staying in a foreign country for more than a few days, you can't (5) _____ be critical of everything around you. It'll make your life miserable.
The greatest divider of nations is ignorance, and so the first solution is knowledge. We recommend that you (6) _____ as much as you can about the host culture before you arrive – its customs, people, priorities and manners. When you've done your homework, if you really can't imagine (7) _____ a new life there, go somewhere else.
We also encourage you (8) _____ the attitude that diversity is interesting. No one would really want to live in a world in which every culture is the same, so we'd (9) _____ to observe and enjoy the differences. Eventually you will come to accept them.
We look forward (10) _____ from you about your experiences.

How to ... | give advice/make recommendations about places

4 Match the sentence halves.
1. The Taj Mahal really is a must- ☐
2. Disney World is superb value ☐
3. The hotel is nice, but it's ☐
4. Everyone says the museum is amazing, but in my view it's not ☐
5. If I were you, I'd ☐
6. You should try ☐
7. Make sure ☐
8. Watch out ☐
9. One thing to be wary ☐
10. Whatever you ☐

a. for mosquitoes and take your malaria pills.
b. backpacking because it's cheap.
c. of is the number of pickpockets.
d. see because it's so beautiful.
e. all it's cracked up to be.
f. go in April when isn't too hot.
g. do, don't miss the textiles market.
h. a bit overpriced.
i. you go to the Eiffel Tower.
j. for money.

Vocabulary | being polite

5 a Rewrite the sentences using the words in brackets.
1. Can you turn down the music? (mind)
   Would _____ down the music?
2. You really ought to accept that offer. (were)
   If _____ , I'd accept that offer.
3. Can you hand in your essay first thing tomorrow? (think)
   _____ you could hand in your essay first thing tomorrow?
4. Can I come? (possible)
   Would _____ for me to come?
5. Ideally, you could help us move our things out of the house. (hoping)
   We _____ you could help us move our things out of the house.
6. I don't know if you can retake those exams, but I doubt it. (thought)
   I _____ you can retake.

b 2.2 Listen and repeat the sentences.

13

2.2

Grammar | comparatives

1 a Read texts 1 and 2 and complete the sentence.

Text 1 is _____ positive about Wikipedia _____ Text 2.

for your information ...
We question the facts so you know the truth

1

Wikipedia has revolutionised the way encyclopaedias are compiled. Its open nature has led to a democratising process; knowledge is now not only in the hands of professors, but of the ordinary man or woman who has the interest, time and dedication to research and document facts. No wonder the establishment feels threatened. 'It's not authoritative!' they cry. 'It's too left-wing!' 'It doesn't represent the whole range of culture!' Of course it doesn't. It is a contemporary comment on the world. With time, today's contributors' views will be challenged and edited by a new generation.

2

Wikipedia is a valuable resource for the amateur researcher in a hurry. If you want to find out when the Crimean War started, or what *quarks* are or when Picasso painted *Guernica*, Wikipedia will tell you, with 99.99 percent accuracy. But for anything more complex Wikipedia is full of potential or real misinformation. It's not the contributors' fault; they genuinely want to get it right. But, for all we know, the contributors could be five-year-olds. Wikipedia's open-source system means that anyone – young children, obsessives and the lunatic fringe – can edit it. Because of this, no serious academic should trust Wikipedia.

next week we discuss ...

b Find and correct the mistake in each sentence.
1 It is nothing near as complimentary about Wikipedia as the other text.
2 It suggests that Wikipedia is nowhere like as reliable as other encyclopaedias.
3 It is more considerably positive about Wikipedia than the other text.
4 The author of the text had rather let each generation question the views of the preceding generation.
5 According to the text, the less we know about the contributors, less we can trust Wikipedia.
6 The author of the text is definitely not as critical of Wikipedia to the author of the other text.
7 The author of the text probably thinks that rather for using Wikipedia for all research, you should only use it for simple facts.
8 The text implies that it's a mile better to let everyone contribute to encyclopaedias.

c Are the statements in Ex. 1b about Text 1 or Text 2?

How to ... | recognise informal writing

2 a Replace the words/expressions in *italics* with words/expressions from the box. You don't need all of them.

in due course   don't hesitate to contact me
would like   concerning   Dear   be grateful
Yours sincerely   of your attendance
following   a previous arrangement
look forward to hearing   take place

☐ 1 We *hope to hear* from you *soon*.
_____
☐ 2 Please *get in touch* if you have any queries.
_____
☐ 3 *Hi* Mrs Dormer,
_____
☐ 4 Technics Solutions *wants* to invite you to our annual investors' meeting
_____
☐ 5 inform us *whether you will be able to come* by 14th June.
_____
☐ 6 which will *be* at The Atrium on Rose Street at 5.00 p.m. on Wednesday 6th July.
_____
☐ 7 We would *like it* if you could
_____
☐ 8 *Best wishes*,
_____

b Number the sentences in the correct order to make a formal letter.

14

Reading

3 **a** Read the texts. Which community did each website target?

a Fashionable people ☐
b Readers ☐
c People who have goods to sell ☐

1
Pierre Omidyar, the son of French-Iranian immigrants, was already a millionaire before launching eBay. Omidyah's electronics site, e-shop, was bought out by Microsoft in 1996, making him a millionaire before he'd turned thirty. With this money, he set up an online auction company which allowed people to show items they wished to sell; other users then made a bid. Omidyar wanted to name the site Echo Bay Technology Group, but this name was already owned by a Canadian mining company, so he shortened the name to eBay, and a legend was born. Almost immediately eBay made a profit. The site sold goods ranging from computers to posters to underwear. The growth of eBay was phenomenal. It is now the world's most successful online business and its users consider themselves part of a distinct community. 150 million registered users buy and sell goods worth $1,050 every second. The website is used by big companies such as Vodaphone and IBM to sell off excess stock, but the majority of goods still sell for less than $50.

2
It was the early 90s, the Internet boom was just beginning, and Jeff Bezos wanted to be a part of this brave, new, forward-thinking community. After leaving his job on Wall Street, Bezos decided to set up an online bookselling business. Using his garage in Seattle as an office, Bezos created Amazon.com. The idea was to make the buying of books cheap and easy, with more choice than the traditional bookshop could provide. The site had a number of features which made it attractive to potential users: fast service, search capabilities, low costs for users, tools for comparing prices of books, and personalisation in the form of customer-written book reviews. As a twenty-four hour virtual bookshop, Amazon was convenient, cheap and reliable. Gradually, through word-of-mouth, the company grew in popularity. Bezos had originally handled customer orders himself, but soon he realised that the company was growing too fast for one man. By 1998 the net sales were $540 million and a whole generation of book buyers was hooked.

3
Ernst Malmsten, an events organiser, and Kajsa Leander, a supermodel, grew up in Lund, Sweden. In the late 90s, they decided to launch boo.com, a website that would create a global fashion community by selling designer clothes all over the world.

From the beginning there were difficulties. Clothing companies didn't trust the Internet and were reluctant to sell online. Also, no one was sure that people would buy clothes without trying them on first. On 3rd November 1999, the day boo.com was launched, the website had 25,000 hits, but these resulted in only eight actual orders for clothes. Worse, a well-known journalist wrote a negative article about boo.com, explaining how it had taken him eighty-one minutes to order a product. Other problems included viruses and a fraud detection system that rejected customers' orders. By March 2000, half of boo.com's workforce had lost their jobs. While most Internet start-ups are run from garages or bedrooms, boo.com had luxurious offices in six of the world's most glamorous and expensive cities. Fresh fruit and flowers were delivered daily. Malmsten and Leander, who always travelled first-class, claimed that companies in the fashion industry needed this image. But boo.com was spending faster than it was earning, and the company was doomed.

b Are these statements true about eBay, Amazon.com or boo.com?

1 The founder originally wanted a different name for the website. _____
2 The company had a high-class, stylish image. _____
3 Users of the site could post their own opinions of the things being sold. _____
4 The site sold a range of goods from the beginning. _____
5 The type of goods for sale weren't ideal for online shopping. _____
6 The founder/founders originally ran the website alone. _____
7 The founder/founders was/were already rich before launching the website. _____
8 The company had some technical problems. _____

c Find words in the texts that mean:

1 offer of a price for something (v, n) (Text 1) _____
2 extraordinary or remarkable (adj) (Text 1) _____
3 a store of goods ready for sale (n) (Text 1) _____
4 unwilling/not wanting to do something (adj) (Text 3) _____
5 new company (especially Internet companies) (n) (Text 3) _____
6 extremely comfortable and expensive (adj) (Text 3) _____
7 destined to end badly or in failure (adj) (Text 3) _____

2.3

Listening

1 a 2.3 Cover the tapescript. Listen to three speakers talking about their communities. What positive aspects of each community do they talk about?

Positive aspects:
Speaker 1 _____
Speaker 2 _____
Speaker 3 _____

TAPESCRIPT

1

People might think that because the community is poor, the people are incredibly unhappy or maybe there's nothing to do. But that's really not the case at all. All kinds of things go on within the townships, so you'd say it was a real hive of activity. For example, one of the ways we entertain ourselves is through music, and if you think about it, you'll understand that music brings people together and of course it's free. There are so many choirs here I've lost count, and they don't just sing our traditional songs; they do all sorts of other things like pop and classical music. A traveller once left us a tape of Robbie Williams and we learned these songs and sing the harmonies. Another activity that's important here is football. Again, the beauty of it is that it's free and anyone can play. The girls have a team, and there's an over-sixties team. The main pitch used to be covered with broken glass and animals grazing, but we fixed it and now it's very good. And whenever Bafana Bafana plays, we all sit around one television and cheer and sing. So, life in a township is hard, of course, but we have a way of making the best out of the things we have. No one sits around feeling sorry for himself.

2

My grandfather once told me a saying. He said that the land doesn't belong to the people; the people belong to the land. I think this idea is one of the reasons why Vanuatu is special. The people are close to nature, and the nature here really is wonderful. Vanuatu is made up of lots of small islands, and we have beautiful coastlines and rainforests. The land is so fertile that we grow most of our own food, and this means that even the many poor people here won't starve. We are a close-knit community. People tend to help each other perhaps more than in built-up, developed communities.
I remember a few years ago an Englishman was stranded on one of the islands with his ten-year-old son because of a problem with the airline. I think he was a researcher. There were no shops or hotels, but the people here fed them and looked after them for three weeks until they could fly out. This is quite normal in Vanuatu. We are a spiritual people, not very materialistic. We enjoy what we have and don't really seek material things. I hope that is how the world sees us, although I'm told that we are more famous for inventing bungee jumping!

3

We were fed up of the … I guess you could call them 'annoyances' of living in a regular community, so we decided to set up our own. Four years ago a group of twenty-eight of us, all retired and all over sixty-five, bought up some real estate and had the whole community designed and laid out for us. And this is the result. We have nothing at all against young people. In fact, most of us have children and grandchildren. But as a place to live, we just wanted a quiet neighbourhood without the noise and the trash, and it works incredibly well. We are all old friends and we have complementary skills, like Jack down the road knows how to service an automobile, and I used to work in property law so I deal with those issues. Reuben Barrios next door was a gardener so he tells everyone how to grow flowers. It's everything we wanted from our old age. The grandchildren visit us on the weekend and we have a lot of fun, but come Monday they're gone and it's back to a quiet life.

b Mark the statements true (T) or false (F). Listen again to check.

Speaker 1
1 The speaker is from a rich area. ☐
2 The hobbies they do don't cost anything. ☐
3 The people of the community are probably close and they do many things together. ☐

Speaker 2
4 Vanuatu is a place of natural beauty. ☐
5 Most of the people of Vanuatu are wealthy. ☐
6 The speaker thinks that the people of Vanuatu are becoming more materialistic. ☐

Speaker 3
7 The speaker is probably quite wealthy. ☐
8 The community is made up of friends. ☐
9 The speaker wishes there were more young people in the community. ☐

c Choose the best definition. Look at the tapescript to help you.

Speaker 1
1 a real hive of activity
   A full of action and productivity
   B a place where people meet
   C an appropriate time to do something
2 Bafana Bafana
   A an African game
   B a football team
   C a type of music

Speaker 2
3 fertile
   A beautiful and full of colour
   B free for everyone to use
   C good for growing plants/food
4 stranded
   A very hungry
   B in trouble with the police
   C couldn't get out

Speaker 3
5 real estate
   A a very large house
   B a plan made by an architect
   C property such as houses or land
6 complementary (adj)
   A saying how good something is
   B the best
   C (things) go well together, though they are different

Vocabulary | describing places

2 Complete the text with words from the box.

off the beaten track   unspoilt   diverse
tranquil   heart   side by side   vast
run-down   stunning   packed   gaze   stroll

Jill and Werner's Travel blog across Eastern Europe

Instead of going to the usual tourist spots, Werner and I went (1) _____ to Tallinn, capital of Estonia. I'm glad we did. The (2) _____ of the city is the Old Town. We found the architecture absolutely (3) _____ with cobbled streets and church spires, castles and beautiful ancient buildings standing (4) _____ . We wandered for a while before stopping for lunch in a local restaurant. I ate a superb cod and potato dish while Werner tucked into a lamb cutlet.

The best thing to do in Tallinn is to (5) _____ at the old buildings – the (6) _____ town hall, which seems to stretch for miles, and the wonderful Alexander Nevsky Cathedral. It's a great city to (7) _____ around because everything is fairly close together and the streets are pedestrian-friendly.

We were staying in a very cheap hotel near the centre. The building was old and slightly (8) _____ and the room wasn't the biggest, but it was clean and comfortable. In the evening we went out to sample the nightlife. I was told that the clubbing scene is pretty (9) _____ , with techno, jazz, folk and disco music all available every night of the week. Tallinn is also becoming popular with the stag party crowd and apparently some of the nightclubs – Hollywood and Decolte in particular – are usually (10) _____ with tourists. But when we were there, the town seemed completely (11) _____ by tourism. Werner and I went for a quiet drink in a bar called Guitar Safari, and ended up listening to excellent live music all evening. Overall, after the excitement of some of the other cities, we found our experience of Tallinn extremely (12) _____ , but by no means boring.

Review and consolidation unit 2

Vocabulary

1 Choose the correct alternative.

1. The problem with Monaco is that the *price/cost/rate* of living is so high.
2. The transport *structure/facility/infrastructure* is good in London.
3. Germany has a *mild/calm/normal* climate. It isn't boiling in summer or freezing in winter.
4. The *health/medical/healthcare* system in Cuba used to be excellent, with many top hospitals.
5. Arguably, the highest *standard/rate/style* of living is found in Scandinavian countries.
6. For several years the crime *level/statistics/rate* in New York has been falling.
7. *Job opportunities/Job-seeking/Unemployment* among unqualified immigrants has long been a problem in France.
8. Apart from the air *uncleanness/pollution/dirt*, Mexico City is wonderful.
9. In most countries there is far less racial *danger/worry/tension* than there used to be.
10. In almost all major cities there are dangerous *no-go/don't-go/mustn't-go* areas.
11. The best thing about Barcelona is its fantastic cultural *story/life/style*.
12. The *party life/night action/nightlife* in Poland is fantastic.
13. Hong Kong is becoming increasingly *cosmopolitan/diverse/varied*.
14. The best thing about Brazil is the sense of *liberty/freeing/freedom* as you walk around.
15. Egypt has possibly the world's most amazing *monuments/artefacts/buildings*, such as the pyramids.
16. In most city centres there's a lot of traffic *pollution/congestion/excess*.

Verb patterns

2 Add words and phrases from the box to complete the sentences. You will not need all of them.

```
to watch    recommend   entering    being
us to use   to do       afford      going    stand
to go       avoids      of watching   us using
to pass     is          urge       us to enter   doing
```

1. I'm thinking of to France. What's the weather like in April?
2. Dave can't to take a holiday, so he's camping in his garden this year!
3. Can you imagine an astronaut? You could go into space!
4. Mario's so lazy: he always doing the washing-up.
5. I tried to persuade Gail a DVD tonight, but she didn't want to.
6. I can't smoking; cigarette smoke makes me ill.
7. They advised traveller's cheques because they're safer.
8. I wouldn't spending more than an hour or two in that museum. It's a bit dull.
9. My teachers always encouraged me my best.
10. Libby urged the competition. She was right: we won!

Comparatives

3 Complete the text. Add eight words.

The online community is predicting that blogs will soon replace print journalism. While publishing news and views on the web is far easier *than* getting into print, I have my doubts about this prediction. Firstly, blogs are nowhere as reliable as print journalism. There are checks and balances for print journalists, and newspapers are far likely than websites to be prosecuted if they get the facts wrong. Reading a blog is much the same reading a diary: if it is full of lies and exaggeration, there's not a lot you can do. The advantage of blogs is that they are personal and usually unedited. But than using them as formal carriers of news, I think we'd be better having them as an alternative source of opinion. Basically, they act as a voice that cannot be silenced. The easier the web becomes to use, more diverse voices it will contain, and that's a great thing. As for me, I sooner read a newspaper any day!

4 Do the pairs of sentences have similar (S) or different (D) meanings?

1. A It's much the same whether you buy your ticket on the Internet or at the station.
   B Buying the ticket on the Internet is marginally cheaper but there's hardly any difference. ☐
2. A I'd sooner live in a quiet community than one with lots of nightlife.
   B In my view, the more nightlife, the better. ☐
3. A São Paulo is much the biggest city I've ever been in.
   B São Paulo is by far the biggest city I've ever been in. ☐
4. A The less we mix with that community, the less trouble we'll have.
   B We're much better off mixing with that community. ☐
5. A Togo is nowhere near as expensive as South Africa.
   B South Africa is nothing like as cheap as Togo. ☐
6. A Lugano is considerably prettier than my home town.
   B My home town isn't quite as pretty as Lugano. ☐
7. A Bristol is nothing like as exciting as the town where I grew up.
   B Bristol is miles more exciting than the town where I grew up. ☐
8. A I'd prefer us to live in the countryside than the city.
   B I think we'd be better off living in the countryside than the city. ☐

Vocabulary

5 Complete the crossword with the missing words.

Across
1. That jacket you bought ten years ago was good _____ for money. It still looks nice.
2. When you go to the market be _____ of pickpockets. They are notorious.
3. Everyone said the film was great but I thought it was a bit _____ .
4. That statue isn't all it's _____ up to be. I thought it would be much more beautiful than it is.

Down
3. You should watch _____ for the mosquitoes. There are a lot of them at this time of year.
5. The drinks are _____ in this nightclub. They shouldn't be this expensive!
7. You can't miss the Picasso exhibition. It's a _____ !
8. The film was really _____ . I found it so boring that I fell asleep.

6 Put the letters in *italics* in the correct order to make words and phrases.

The town where I grew up used to be absolutely (1) *hcraginm*. The scenery was (2) *rnqtluai*: there were large rolling hills and a small forest (3) *fof het nebaet rktac*. I used to (4) *slrtol* there for hours on end, and (5) *azge* at the trees. I went back there recently and was surprised at how much it had changed. Right in the (6) *threa* of the town there was a car park which stood (7) *dise yb edis* with a new shopping mall. I went inside the mall and it was (8) *ecakpd*. Then I drove to my old school, which was still (9) *gutibsln* with children, though the buildings looked a little (10) *nru nwod*. I went in, hoping to see some of my old teachers, when suddenly a security guard approached, asked who I was, and promptly kicked me out. So I drove towards the forest, assuming that some things would remain (11) *poutnlsi*. Unfortunately, the forest didn't exist any more: they'd built a (12) *asvt* block of flats there.

7 Choose the correct words and phrases to finish the sentences.

1. Alexandra cycles so fast that she's extremely hard to keep
   A on with. B up to. C up with.
2. The work was tough but we were able to carry it
   A out. B by. C in.
3. A solution to this problem won't be easy, but we'll see what we manage to come
   A round for. B in to. C up with.
4. The house was very run down so we had to do it
   A round. B up. C over.
5. Hannah has just started at a new school, so I hope she fits
   A in. B up. C on.
6. It'll be a great party if he turns
   A up. B on. C out.
7. There was a crash on the motorway so the traffic was held
   A in. B up. C on.
8. The salary is terrible. They barely pay you enough money to get
   A through. B on. C by.

19

3.1 Tales

Reading

1 a Read the article and choose the best summary.

1 Some communities claim they have a secret way to stay young and healthy. The article describes how they manage to do it.
2 Some communities claim that many of their people live until they are over a hundred. The article disputes these claims.
3 Some researchers believe that ancient communities are healthier than modern societies. The article lists the problems of modern living.

b Read the article again. Write questions for these answers.

1 It was an academic paper about the peoples he studied.
2 A local man whose stated age changed by eleven years in only four years.
3 It was lost when a church caught fire.
4 Because in these societies, the older you are, the more respected you are.
5 The condition of the people's bones, and official documents.
6 Because they were afraid of being caught.

The old age hoax

A little old man walks the fields of Vilcabamba, Ecuador. His skin is wrinkled from exposure to the sun, and his legs move slowly, steadily. As the sky turns red, he puts down his ancient tools and walks across the valley to the mud hut that he calls home. He is 140 years old.

Hard to believe? Well, Methuselah lived to be 969, according to the Bible. And, according to some, there are communities – the people of Vilcabamba, the Abkhazians of Georgia, the Hunza of Pakistan – which contain large numbers of centenarians, those lucky people who live to be 100.

Let's take a trip back in time. January,1973. Dr Alexander Leaf of Harvard University publishes a report in the *National Geographic* magazine that describes his journeys to study the Hunza, Abkhazians and the Vilcabambas. He calls his report *Every Day Over 100 is a Gift*. According to Leaf, there are ten times the number of centenarians found in these areas than is normal in modern Western civilisations. The article caused a minor stir in anthropology circles and one or two commercial ones too: an American entrepreneur makes plans to invest in bottled water from Vilcabamba, and a Japanese company discusses building a hotel there for elderly tourists.

But then, as further studies followed Leaf's, the evidence began to point not to mythical communities with ancient youth-preserving lifestyles, but rather to lies, exaggeration and the creation of a sensational myth. Although Leaf's report sounded plausible enough at first, a number of questions arose later. When Dr Leaf returned to Vilcabamba four years after his first visit, one of the villagers, Miguel Carpiro, had miraculously become eleven years older. Leaf asked to see Carpiro's birth certificate, but was told that it had been destroyed in a church fire.

Indeed, birth records were one of the main problems: societies with low levels of literacy usually don't have them. And in Vilcabamba names were used repeatedly within the family so that grandfathers, fathers and sons may have exactly the same name, adding to the confusion. Furthermore, old age is revered in societies such as Abkhazian, and so people exaggerate to improve their social status. When the exaggeration also brings about increased attention and tourism, there is even further temptation to add a few years to your age.

After Leaf's report, two researchers, Mazess and Forman, went to Vilcabamba and checked skeletal conditions as well as existing records. They found enormous inaccuracies everywhere. Miguel Carpiro, who had claimed to be 121, was actually eighty-seven. His mother was born five years after he'd claimed to be born! Another researcher, a Russian geneticist named Zhores Medvedev, studied the people of Abkhazia, who had also claimed to have many centenarians. He discovered that many of them had assumed the identities of their parents. Some of these people were World War I deserters, and they had used their dead parents' names in order to avoid detection.

So, myth or reality? We don't know for sure. Roger Maupin, an anthropologist, says of these peoples: 'Their lifestyle is certainly healthy. They have constant steady work, a good diet and a small community untroubled by such things as war, technology and the stresses these bring. But we just have no reliable evidence about their real age. Ultimately, I don't think it matters. It's not the age you live to, it's the quality of your life that counts.'

c Underline words/phrases in the article that mean:
1 people who are still alive at 100 (n) (line 10)
2 attracted a lot of attention (v) (line 18)
3 believable (adj) (line 27)
4 deeply respected (adj) (line 38)
5 importance (how much a person is respected) within a community (n) (line 40)
6 causes (v) (line 41)
7 soldiers who run away from battle (n) (line 53)
8 being found (v) (line 55)

Grammar | narrative tenses

2 Tick the sentences that describe the pictures.

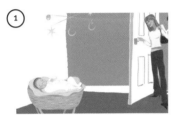 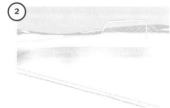

1 At midnight, when we got back, she had already put the baby to bed.
At midnight, when we got back, she was putting the baby to bed.
2 The game was cancelled because it had been snowing.
The game was cancelled because it was snowing.
3 Juan had painted the bathroom.
Juan had been painting the bathroom.
4 I got home and discovered that my flat had been burgled.
I got home and discovered that my flat was being burgled.
5 Junichi told us he had been training for the Olympics.
Junichi told us he was training for the Olympics.
6 When I saw Joan she was going to the hairdresser.
When I saw Joan she had been to the hairdresser.

3 Complete the sentences using the correct forms of the verbs in brackets.
1 Who _____ to on the phone? (talk)
2 We could tell from his filthy clothes that he _____ in the garden for hours. (work)
3 I knew something was wrong because the dog _____ constantly. (bark)
4 How _____ me? I thought I was safe. (find)
5 Once I _____ her properly, I knew she was the girl for me. (meet)
6 The maid obviously hadn't come because my room _____ . (clean)
7 _____ of him before you saw the film? (hear)
8 Later, I realised that we _____ about different people! (talk)
9 I couldn't pick him up because my car _____ in the garage. (fix)
10 It was clear that he _____ anything during the lecture. (understand)

Pronunciation

4 **3.1** Cover the tapescript. Listen and tick (✓) the sentences you hear.
1 A I'd have helped you every time. ☐
  B I've helped you every time. ☐
2 A Why did you hit him? ☐
  B Why had you hit him? ☐
3 A Have we paid already? ☐
  B Had we paid already? ☐
4 A Would you like to play chess? ☐
  B Do you like to play chess? ☐
5 A I'd run ten miles. ☐
  B I've run ten miles. ☐
6 A She'd stopped smoking. ☐
  B She stopped smoking. ☐
7 A I prefer vegetables to meat. ☐
  B I'd prefer vegetables to meat. ☐
8 A I hadn't run for ages. ☐
  B I didn't run for ages. ☐

TAPESCRIPT
1 I'd have helped you every time.
2 Why had you hit him?
3 Had we paid already?
4 Would you like to play chess?
5 I've run ten miles.
6 She'd stopped smoking.
7 I'd prefer vegetables to meat.
8 I hadn't run for ages.

3.2

Reading and Listening

1. **a** 🔊 3.2 Read and listen to a short story. Answer the questions.

   1. Who do you think had the idea to go birdwatching?
   2. What type of town do Thomas and Rosie live in?
   3. Is Thomas good at spelling? How do we know?
   4. What type of person is Rosie? How do we know?
   5. What does the father think of Thomas's description of the birdwatching trip?
   6. Why was Rosie 'disgraced'?
   7. How does the father feel about his children?
   8. Which of these words would you use to describe the story? Circle one or more of the words.

   surprising   surreal   traditional
   shocking   funny

   b Find words in the text that mean:
   1. ready and waiting (line 9) (*adj*) _____
   2. high-pitched shout (line 20) (*n*) _____
   3. walking with short steps, body moving from side to side (line 32) (*v*) _____
   4. walking vigorously (usually through something) (line 34) (*v*) _____
   5. preserved in some kind of (solid) form, but no longer living/growing/used (line 35) (*adj*) _____
   6. thrown away/abandoned (line 42) (*adj*) _____
   7. made something uneven/messy by rubbing it (line 42) (*v*) _____
   8. looking at something, angrily (line 49) (*v*) _____

   c Find the object or person in the text that these words refer to.
   1. it (line 4) _____
   2. on which (line 10) _____
   3. this same sound (line 25) _____
   4. it (line 27) _____
   5. It (line 31) _____
   6. it (line 33) _____
   7. he (line 47) _____
   8. its (line 48) _____

Birdwatcher

At 2.32 on the afternoon of 10th July, eight-year-old Thomas Smith saw a large yellow-beaked eagle rise from the roof of the local post office. His sister, ten-year-old Rosie, didn't see it because she was busy
5   applying her mother's lipstick to her small, but very pretty, mouth, and in any case she wasn't all that keen on birdwatching.
   'Rosie,' said Thomas. 'How do you spell eagle?' His pencil was poised above a notebook which
10 had a picture of an owl on the front and on which Thomas had written 'BuRds'. B-u-r-d-s.
   'Eagle?' said Rosie. 'I-d-i-o-t.'
   'Very funny.'
   'E-e-g-l-e.'
15 Thomas wrote it down. Eegle. 2.32, 10th July. Kingston Road Post Office.
   They crossed the street, slipping between the fat cars all stopped still in the summer heat, fingers tapping outside windows. It was at this point that
20 Thomas heard the distant shriek of seagulls and recognised the sound at once. The previous summer they had spent a week with their parents at a seaside town eating huge sausages in pools of grease and getting red-faced in the sun, and had been woken
25 every morning by this same sound.
   'Rosie, how do you spell seagull?'
   'Same as eagle but it starts with an s.'
   At 2.58 Thomas and Rosie paused for a minute while Rosie searched her handbag for the blue eye
30 shadow that she had removed from her mother's drawer. It was called Aquamarine Dream. At this moment, Thomas noticed a penguin waddling down the High Street. Thomas watched it go by, the penguin merrily traipsing through the cigarette butts
35 and chewing gum stains fossilised on the pavement, and Thomas wrote 'Pen Win' in his notebook.
   Later, while the disgraced Rosie was shut up in her room, her mother's makeup returned, Thomas sat at his father's feet and explained about the eagle
40 on the post office roof, the ostrich outside the library, the vulture in Rosemary Gardens snacking on a discarded bag of popcorn. And his father ruffled the boy's hair and laughed to himself and thought about the wonders of the child's imagination. And
45 the man felt at peace with the world and with his two naughty children, at least until 3.11 a.m. the following morning when he was woken by an enormous white swan sitting at the end of his bed, its yellow eyes glaring.

22

Vocabulary | describing books

2 Complete the book review using words from the box.

> depicts one-dimensional down turner
> base account found hooked bestseller
> bookworm gripping avid

Meredith Johnson's new book, *Feather Man*, like her four previous novels, is a (1) page-_____ and destined to be a (2) _____ . Unusually for Johnson, she doesn't (3) _____ her plot on a true story (her last book was a fictionalised (4) _____ of a failed bank robbery), though once again she brilliantly (5) _____ Edinburgh's criminal underworld, where a wrong word can earn you a slashing with a razor blade and a wrong move can get you injected with something very nasty indeed.

She soon has the reader (6) _____ . The hero, Paul Schroeder, detective and (7) _____ who spends half his life in a library, finds himself investigating a writer called Max Dowling when Schroeder realises that Dowling leaves clues to unsolved crimes in his books.

I (8) _____ the story totally (9) _____ , and if some of the characters are a little (10) _____ – for example, a rather unrealistic group of street gangsters all seem to wear raincoats, smoke a lot and have particularly unpleasant domestic pets – the pace and action more than make up for it. Frankly, I couldn't put *Feather Man* (11) _____ . I recommend it highly not only for (12) _____ readers of Johnson's work, but for new converts, too.

How to ... | describe people

3 Read what these people say about their partners. Circle the correct alternative.

1. She comes *across/over/around* as very kind and gentle when you first meet her.
2. Once you *become to know/get to know/seem to know* her, you realise she's really funny.
3. The thing that *strikes/hits you/strikes you* about Colin is that he's so intelligent.
4. What I really *think about/like for/like about* Susana is her sense of humour.
5. Matthew is *such a/so/a such* talented guy that you have to admire him.
6. He can be *a bit of/a bit/bit* mean sometimes, especially when he's in a bad mood.

Vocabulary | compound adjectives

4 a Match the compound adjective halves.

1. single- ☐   a minded
2. self-   ☐   b minded
3. thick-   ☐   c offish
4. kind-   ☐   d orientated
5. stand-   ☐   e hearted
6. career- ☐   f skinned
7. level-   ☐   g sufficient
8. absent- ☐   h headed

b Match the compound adjectives in Ex. 4a to the people in these extracts. You may match more than one to each person. Two compound adjectives are not used.

1. Bradbury was determined to claw his way to the top of the company, trampling on whoever got in his way. He had only been in the business six months when he decided that the quickest way to get promoted would be to murder William DeFries.

   _____

2. Delilah sat in the corner for the whole party. Whenever a young man approached, she immediately feigned boredom and continued sipping from her slim glass of iced water, eyes raised to the ceiling.

   _____

3. My mother was the type of person who regularly left home in her slippers. She frequently forgot to turn off ovens, lights, televisions and radios. She was known to make phone calls and, on being answered, immediately forget not only why she was calling, but who she was calling.

   _____

4. Being short, skinny and ugly, I have been called names since I was old enough to walk. 'Stick insect, creepy-crawly, witch, rat-face, alien, ET, lizard.' I answer the name-callers with a wink and a smile. You see, I just don't care.

   _____

5. Mr Trimble had watery grey eyes and a pocket permanently stuffed full of sweets for any children he came across. He walked with the slowness of a snail, leaving no slime but a trail of happiness wherever he went.

   _____

3.3

Listening

1 a [3.3] Cover the tapescript. Listen to three jokes and match the pictures to the jokes.

TAPESCRIPT

1 _____

A policeman stops a car because it is speeding. He asks the driver for his licence. 'I don't have one,' says the driver. 'And the car's not mine. I stole it. But I think I saw a driver's licence in the glove box when I put my gun in there.'

'You stole it?! You have a gun in the glove box?!'

'Yes,' says the driver. 'I put it there just before I threw the car owner's body in the boot.' The policeman calls for backup and five minutes later four police cars arrive. The captain says, 'Sir, may I see your licence?'

'Sure,' says the driver. He opens the glove box slowly and gives him the licence. The police captain says, 'So, no gun in the glove box?'

'Gun? Of course not!'

'And no body in the boot?'

'What?!' says the driver. And the captain says: 'My police officer told me you had a gun in the glove box and a body in the boot.'

'Yeah, and I bet the liar told you I was speeding too.'

2 _____

A couple owned a cat, but the man hated it. So one day he decided to get rid of it. He drove ten blocks and threw the cat out of the car window. But when he got home, there the cat was, lying on the doormat. So the next day he drove twenty blocks and threw the cat into a river. But, on entering his driveway the cat was there again, fast asleep by the door. So the next day he drove fifteen blocks, took a left, took a right, went down the motorway, crossed a couple of bridges and threw the cat into a large hole in the ground. After driving a while, he called his wife. 'Is the cat there?' he asked.

'Yes,' she said. 'Why do you ask?'

'OK, put the cat on the phone. I'm lost and I need directions home.'

3 _____

A new manager walks into his office and finds four numbered envelopes on the desk. Number one says 'Open me first'. So he opens it and finds a letter from the previous manager. It says, 'When the company is having problems and you don't know what to do, open these envelopes in order.' So he puts the envelopes away and forgets about them. Six months later, the company is in big trouble and the manager may lose his job. Suddenly he remembers the envelopes so he opens the second envelope. In it there is a message which says, 'Blame everything on me, the previous manager.' He does this and saves his job and the company recovers. But six months after this, the company is in trouble again and losing money fast. He opens the third envelope and reads the message. It says, 'Blame everything on the government.' He does this and everyone agrees and he keeps his job. Six months later the company is in even bigger trouble, and the workers are on strike. So he opens the fourth envelope. The message says: 'Prepare four envelopes.'

b Complete the sentences from the tapescript. Listen again to check.

Joke 1

1 The driver was stopped because he was _____ .

2 There wasn't a gun in the _____ or a body in the _____ .

Joke 2

3 A man wanted to _____ of a cat.

4 The man needed _____ to get home.

Joke 3

5 The second note said '_____ everything on me'.

6 The manger's final problem was that the workers were on _____ .

c Read the sentences below. Mark the sentences that are sarcastic (SA), show surprise (S) and those which are said calmly (C).

1 'You stole it?! You have a gun in the glove box?!' ___

2 'I put it there just before I threw the car owner's body into the boot.' ___

3 'Sir, may I see your licence?' ___

4 'So no gun in the glove box?' ___

5 'Gun? Of course not!' ___

6 'My police officer told me you had a gun in the glove box and a body in the boot.' ___

7 'Yeah, and I bet the liar told you I was speeding, too.' ___

d Listen again. Answer the questions.

1 Which sentences are said loudly?

2 In which sentences does the voice rise and fall a lot? Which words are emphasised?

3 In which sentences does the tone of voice stay the same?

e Listen again and repeat the sentences.

Grammar | participles/gerunds

2 Six of these sentences contain mistakes. Tick (✓) the correct sentences and correct the mistakes in the others using participles and gerunds.

1. Not having heard the music, I can't really judge it.
2. On been arrested by the police, Teresa admitted that she was guilty of fraud.
3. She broke her leg while to play hockey.
4. He stood there in front of us, desolate, robbed of everything he'd ever owned.
5. To help other people wasn't something that usually made Mrs Davies happy.
6. Having been given the car just the day before, Lucas promptly crashed it.
7. All of the boys, hoped to be football stars, trained for six hours every day.
8. Told by his teacher that he had the ability to pass his exam, Bill finally achieved his goal.
9. Having wake up at 4.00 a.m., we were exhausted by 11.00.
10. After being listening to the speech for four hours, Bianca eventually fell asleep.

3 Complete the stories with the participle or gerund of verbs from the box.

> have/catch ask play celebrate
> call cheat

In the wild old days of cowboys and saloons, (1) _____ at cards was likely to get you killed. (2) _____ cheating in a saloon in 1857, Donald Blewett was shot dead. The men (3) _____ still wanted to finish their game, however, and they needed another player, so they asked a stranger to join them. This stranger then proceeded to win over $4000. (4) _____ to the scene a bit later, the police decided to try and find Donald Blewett's nearest relative. After (5) _____ around to find out the dead man's name, they discovered that the stranger (6) _____ his $4000 jackpot was Blewett's son, who hadn't seen his father for over ten years.

> have/place tell involve bet have/make know

(7) _____ should never have been easier. (8) _____ elaborate plans to cheat, horse owner and politician Horatio Bottomley placed 'the perfect bet' on a horse race in Belgium. He owned all six of the horses (9) _____ in the race and he employed the six English jockeys. After (10) _____ the jockeys the order in which they should finish, Bottomley thought he couldn't lose. However, (11) _____ his bet, he got a surprise. Halfway through the race, a thick fog descended on the course. As a result, the race was declared null and void, with no winner. Bottomley, (12) _____ for his money-making ability, lost a fortune.

Vocabulary | types of humour

4 Complete the crossword.

Across
1. comic drama using unlikely situations and people acting stupidly
2. a funny drawing
3. make something/someone seem ridiculous (often in order to laugh at people who have power)
4. comic moments connected to very serious subjects
5. humour based on extremely strange connections

Down
6. give the impression that something is greater or larger than it really is
7. humorous use of words that sound the same but have different meanings
8. when you say the opposite of what you mean, for a humorous effect

Review and consolidation unit 3

Vocabulary

1 Choose the correct words and phrases.
1. In order to avoid hurting people, I think it's OK to tell
   A a feeble excuse. B a white lie. C a rumour.
2. Advertising writers aren't exactly liars, but they tend to be a bit
   A of a gossip. B exaggerated. C prone to exaggeration.
3. In order to protect the government, for many years the secret was
   A revealed. B concealed. C taken in.
4. We heard the fire alarm, but it turned out to be a
   A rumour. B false. C hoax.
5. Whenever his results were bad, Peter made
   A excuses. B a lie. C a trick.
6. Joanne first told me about it, and then the rumour
   A went. B passed around. C spread.
7. He's always telling stories about other people – he's such a
   A hoaxer. B bareface. C gossip.
8. I should never have trusted her. She played a trick on me and stupidly I was
   A taken in. B barefaced. C taken by.

Narrative tenses review

2 Complete the sentences using the correct form of verbs from the box.

> face   write   memorise   get up   read
> borrow   turn into   drive   make   leave

1. By midday I was really tired, because I _____ on the motorway since 5 a.m.
2. She said all the noise was because the building next door _____ a shopping mall. The work wouldn't be completed until the following May.
3. They desperately wanted to see Francesca, but the janitor told them that she _____ already.
4. One of the children recited the whole story. Apparently, he _____ it for weeks.
5. When I got home, the fridge _____ a weird noise, so I called the engineer.
6. He _____ his autobiography in the months before he died, so although it wasn't finished, we had a good idea of his life story.
7. My friends knew the film had a twist in the tail, but I didn't because I _____ the book.
8. Rob tried to take a photo of Lily, but she _____ the wrong way.
9. Yevgeny was searching for a book in the library, but it _____ already.
10. _____ you _____ early this morning? I thought I heard you scampering around!

Vocabulary

3 Complete the crossword.

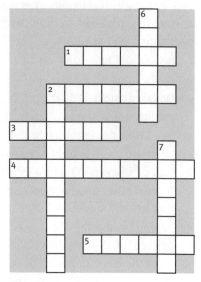

Someone who ...
Across
1. forgets little things is _____-minded.
2. doesn't get offended easily when she is criticised is thick-_____ .
3. is difficult to talk to and not very friendly is stand-_____ .
4. is always thinking about how to get further in her career is career-_____ .
5. is very calm even when in a tricky situation is level-_____ .

Down
2. can look after herself without help is self-_____ .
6. is determined to do something is single-_____ .
7. is generous and nice to others is kind-_____ .

4 Correct the sentences by adding or crossing out one word.
1. Yolanda seems be a very nice girl.
2. You're such fast swimmer, I could never keep up with you.
3. What thing I don't like about Samantha is that she's so selfish.
4. The thing strikes you about Gudrun is her determination.
5. He can be a bit of annoying sometimes, but his heart's in the right place.
6. Once you get to know of Maurice, you'll like him.

26

5 Match the review extracts 1–6 to types of humour from the box. Two are not used.

> farce puns cartoons black humour
> surreal humour irony exaggeration satire

1. Comedian John Weeding spent an hour of his brilliant show doing impressions of Tony Blair and other politicians, and the audience lapped up his hilarious take on modern society.
2. We see the usual tricks of the genre in this tedious play: mistresses hiding in wardrobes, husbands caught with their trousers down, and a plot that goes from the silly to the ridiculous.
3. What animal will always keep you warm? A kangaroo, because it's a good jumper. If you like this type of humour – and most children do – *The Bumper Book of Kids' Jokes* is for you.
4. He goes way beyond what you usually find in the back pages of the newspaper. The writing and drawing are so exquisite that he's been called a mix between Leonardo and Woody Allen.
5. Her whole act is based on creating bizarre combinations. At one point she compares a chocolate cake to the history of space flight, and after the interval she emerges wearing a lobster on her head.
6. The whole play revolves around a search for a dead body. Somehow Lara Williams manages to wring humour out of a very dark situation.

Participle clauses/gerunds

6 Circle the correct alternatives. More than one alternative may be possible.
1. *To hope/Hoping/Hoped* to find a new wife, Davies settled in Paris.
2. *Restored/Having been restored/After restored* to its former glory, the painting was re-hung.
3. *Ran/To run/Running* marathons is what she does best.
4. I know the man *having sat/sat/sitting* in the blue car.
5. *While driving/Driven/Having driven* in the tunnel, keep your lights on.
6. *On hearing/Heard/Having heard* the news, he rushed over to the hospital.
7. *Buried/Being buried/Burying* in the cemetery is a famous scientist of the early twentieth century.
8. *After catching/After being caught/Having been caught*, the robber put down his gun.
9. The photos *taken/being taken/having been taken* today will turn out fine. The light is perfect.
10. *After being treated/Treating/Treated* by experts, the dog began to recover.

Vocabulary

7 Rewrite the sentences using the words in brackets plus two more words.
1. Your current employment has no future prospects and it won't get you anywhere. (dead-end)
   It is _____.
2. Maggie and Denis are always arguing and shouting at each other. (stormy)
   Maggie and Denis have _____.
3. That was the moment when she got promoted and became famous in the industry. (took)
   That was the moment when her _____.
4. The manager is the one who takes responsibility if things go wrong. (line)
   It's the manager who's in _____.
5. They didn't seem at all pleased to see me. (frosty)
   They gave me _____.
6. I'd always wanted to do something different from my mother's work. (footsteps)
   I'd never wanted to follow in _____.
7. Once you get promoted, you'll have to make all the decisions. (shots)
   Once you get promoted, you'll have to _____.
8. He aims to become a fighter pilot. (sights)
   He has his _____ becoming a fighter pilot.
9. We'd come to the point at which we had to make a vital decision. (crossroads)
   We'd _____.
10. Several of us were feeling ill that day. (weather)
    Several of us were feeling a bit _____.

4.1 Progress

Vocabulary | progress

1 **a** Match the words 1–8 to their common collocations a–h.

1 computer a tube
2 skin b company
3 genetic c tissue
4 rare d launch
5 shuttle e strain
6 test f network
7 orbit g the moon
8 software h engineering

b Complete the sentences with collocations from Ex. 1a.

1 Microsoft is a hugely influential _____ .
2 They were able to eradicate the disease through _____ .
3 We watched the _____ on the television. It was incredibly exciting.
4 They used _____ , taken from his leg, to cover the wound.
5 The plan is for the shuttle to _____ the _____ .
6 The cells were placed in a _____ for analysis.
7 Scientists have managed to isolate this very _____ of the virus.
8 I can't use my email. We are having problems with the _____ .

Reading

2 Read the text quickly and choose the best title.
1 Superheroes – too strong for their own good?
2 Real-life superheroes – inspiration for developing superhero character
3 Making a superhero – fact or fiction?

From gamma-radiation to radioactive spiders, superheroes are born in a variety of weird and wonderful ways. But how realistic are they?

Being born on other planets, or finding cosmic lanterns requires a huge leap of the imagination. But what about the humans who develop special powers by slightly more prosaic means – how plausible are they?

Take The Incredible Hulk: Scientist Dr Robert Banner receives a huge dose of gamma rays while working on a nuclear bomb. Gamma rays are real enough, being produced by nuclear explosions, but the bad news is that the gamma-radiation that gave Robert Banner his powers would've only caused fatal radiation sickness.

Forgetting that minor point, Lois Gresh, author of *Science and Superheroes*, argues it's just about possible to create a believable version of hulk. Banner could take large amounts of (highly dangerous) anabolic steroids to produce that pumped-up look, which in real life could cause his notorious rages as they increase aggressive mood swings. As for the green skin, French genetic researchers have at least created a glowing green rabbit by genetic engineering using fluorescent protein.

Spider-Man, on the other hand, has bigger problems. While a radioactive spider could exist (spiders are tolerant to radiation), an animal does not transfer DNA via a bite. And even if it did, it couldn't fuse with our DNA. If being ingested was enough to make this happen, we'd get characteristics of, say, apples or chickens whenever we ate them.

Batman – the 'Dark Knight' – might be the most realistic of the heroes, says Gresh. It is of course possible for a person to train obsessively in martial arts and subjects such as criminology. But in this case, it's gadgets that make Batman who he is. Most of Batman's toys, from his tiny cameras to smoke grenades to superstrong ropes, exist in the 21st century. Even creating a batmobile shouldn't present modern carmakers with too much difficulty.

Grammar | future probability/possibility/certainty

3 Write sentences about the text using the words in brackets.

1. The ... being born on another planet. (odds)
2. I ... you would find a cosmic lantern. (whether)
3. Gamma rays ... produced by nuclear explosions. (definitely)
4. There ... that if Dr Banner had received this radiation, he would have died. (likelihood)
5. There ... we could create a believable version of hulk in reality. (slim)
6. Giving him anabolic steroids would ... create his pumped-up look. (almost)
7. These ... cause him to become more aggressive and moody. (might)
8. There ... that we could create green skin by genetic engineering. (remote)
9. A radioactive spider ... exist. (conceivably)
10. An animal ... of transferring DNA via a bite. (stands)
11. If it did transfer its DNA, it wouldn't ... of fusing with our DNA. (chance)
12. If ingesting DNA was enough to change our own DNA, we ... adopt the characteristics of chickens and apples when we ate them. (presumably)
13. Batman ... be the most realistic of the heroes. (well))
14. There ... that modern carmakers could even create a batmobile. (distinct)

4 Complete the sentences using words from the box.

> doubt against conceivably no likelihood slim
> doubtful well any chances possibility bound

1. A: Do you think there's _____ chance that we'll see Martha at the weekend?
   B: I wouldn't count on it, but there's a _____ chance that she'll turn up.
2. The odds are _____ us meeting the sales targets for this quarter, but there's a strong _____ that things will improve over the coming months.
3. Rooney stands _____ chance of being chosen for the team.
4. I _____ whether they'll finish the work by the end of the week.
5. We may _____ have the chance to explore the area in more detail later.
6. Why did you do that? It's _____ to upset her.
7. It's _____ that they could have chosen a worse time to announce the news.
8. It could _____ help us in the future.
9. There's every _____ that soon he will hand over to his deputy.
10. The _____ are that we'll beat them in the Cup Final.

Listening

5 a 🔊 4.1 Cover the tapescript. Listen to the news programme and answer the questions.

1. Why does the young boy call Leisa 'Wonder Woman'?
2. Why did Nathan Peters climb up the side of the house?

b Listen again and complete the texts.

Real-life superheroes

Leisa Hodgkinson of Warrington is just (1) _____ , but she lifted a (2) _____ off a seven-year-old boy (3) _____ . The boy was (4) _____ , but has since made a (5) _____ and now calls Leisa 'Wonder Woman'. She said at the time that she (6) _____ to lift the car after (7) _____ , the same age as the trapped boy.

Sussex man Nathan Peters won (8) _____ from the Fire Brigade for (9) _____ in 2000 after helping to (10) _____ from a burning building in a (11) _____ worthy of Spider-Man. He scaled the (12) _____ , despite minimal hand and foot-holds, and stayed (13) _____ with the two to comfort them until (14) _____ .

TAPESCRIPT

Leisa Hodgkinson of Warrington is just 1.7 metres tall, but she lifted a one-tonne car off a seven-year-old boy trapped underneath. The boy was severely injured, but has since made a good recovery and now calls Leisa 'Wonder Woman'. She said at the time that she found the strength to lift the car after thinking of her own son, the same age as the trapped boy.

Sussex man Nathan Peters won an award from the Fire Brigade for outstanding bravery in 2000, after helping to rescue a mother and child from a burning building in a daring climb worthy of Spider-Man. He scaled the front of the building, despite minimal hand and foot-holds, and stayed in the smoke-filled room with the two to comfort them until the fire-fighters arrived.

4.2

Vocabulary | talking about plans/free time

1 Choose the correct words to complete the sentences.

1 I'm not at all sure what to do this weekend. I'm really at a loose _____ .
   A time   B end   C up

2 What are you _____ to later? We're going out for a meal.
   A up   B in   C on

3 Have you got anything _____ up for tonight?
   A straight   B going   C lined

4 We *were* planning to all meet for lunch next week, but the plans have fallen _____ .
   A off   B out   C through

5 I'm afraid I'm _____ up all week sorting out the accounts.
   A tied   B turned   C lined

6 Please try and come. Can't you _____ out of going to see your granny?
   A go   B come   C get

7 They've had to call _____ the wedding because she's changed her mind.
   A on   B of   C off

8 I'll let you know if anything else crops _____ .
   A up   B on   C in

9 Do you know if the meeting is still going _____ ?
   A for   B ahead   C in

10 You need to just relax and put your feet _____ .
   A on   B down   C up

Grammar | future tenses review

2 Choose the correct alternative.

1 The traffic's worse than I was expecting. I think we *'re going to/'ll* be late.

2 *I'll/I'm going to* pick you up from the airport if you like.

3 I've got a doctor's appointment this afternoon, so *I'm leaving/I leave* work at 3 p.m.

4 What sort of job do you think you *will do/will be doing* in ten years' time?

5 By the time we get there, all the food *will go/will have gone*.

6 I'm sure you'll have a great time wherever *you decide/you'll decide* to go.

7 He asked if we *will/would* take this case for him.

8 The reception is bad in here. I *'ll/'m going to* call you back in a minute.

9 He's not coming until Thursday, and we *'ll be finishing/'ll have finished* by then.

10 The flight *leaves/is going to leave* at 21.20.

Reading

3 Read the text. Mark the statements true (T) or false (F).

'Slow movement' encourages less stressful living

(1) Carl Honoré, a recovered 'speedaholic', had an epiphany that caused him to slow down the hectic pace of his life. A journalist based in London, Honoré read a newspaper article on time-saving tips that referenced a book of one-minute bedtime stories. He found it an appealing idea since he'd already got into the habit of speed-reading stories to his son. 'My first reaction was, yes, one-minute bedtime stories,' he said. 'My next thought was, whoa, has it really come to this? That was really when a light bulb went off in my head.'

(2) He realised he had become so anxious to rush through the nightly ritual that he'd rather get seven or even eight stories done in less time than he'd normally spend reading one. He wasn't making the most of this quality time.

(3) So he embarked on finding a way to address the issue of 'time poverty', the constant fast-forward motion in which many overscheduled, stressed-out people are always rushing towards their next task – work, meals, family time – rather than savouring what they consider most important.

(4) Honoré's book, *In Praise of Slowness: How a Worldwide Movement Is Challenging the Cult of Speed*, has made him the unofficial godfather of a growing cultural shift towards slowing down. '[There's a] backlash against the mainstream dictate that faster is always better, which puts quantity always ahead of quality,' he said. 'People all across the West are waking up to the folly of that.'

(5) For advocates of the Slow Movement, it's not about rejecting technology or changing modern life completely, but rather about keeping it all in balance – not talking on the phone, driving and checking a BlackBerry while headed to the drive-thru before the next meeting.

'I love technology. I love speed. You need some things to be fast – ice hockey, squash, a fast Internet connection,' Honoré said. 'But,' he said, 'my passion for speed had become an addiction. I was doing everything faster.'

(6) **What to Do?**

To make the transition to a slower life, Honoré has several suggestions: don't schedule something in every free moment of your day – prioritise activities and cut from the bottom of the list; limit television watching; and keep an eye on your 'personal speedometer' so you can gauge when you are rushing for speed's sake rather than necessity.

(7) But don't expect the change to happen immediately – or even naturally. 'You don't slow down by snapping you're fingers, "Now I'm slow"', said Honoré, who got a speeding ticket on his way to a Slow Food dinner as he researched the book. 'That happens,' he said. 'My life has been transformed by it, but I still feel that old itch.'

1 Carl Honoré came to a slow realisation that he was living life too fast. ☐
2 He was reading an article about ways to spend more quality time with your children. ☐
3 Carl initially thought that one-minute bedtime stories were a good idea, as he regularly read stories to his son. ☐
4 He reflected that he needed to re-address the priorities in his life. ☐
5 According to the article, people are stressed because they fail to think ahead to the next task. ☐
6 Carl believes that people are starting to question whether quality is better than quantity. ☐
7 People who join the Slow Movement do not use computers, travel in cars, or watch television. ☐
8 Carl thinks the change to a 'slower' philosophy can only happen slowly. ☐
9 His advice is to reduce the number of things you do by deciding what is least important. ☐
10 He says his life is not so different to before. ☐

4 a Underline words or phrases in the text that mean:
1 desperate (to do something) (*adj*) (para 2)
2 began (something long and difficult) (*v*) (para 3)
3 enjoying (*v*) (para 3)
4 person to whom people look to for advice or (*n*) (para 4)
5 a strong negative reaction (*adj*) (para 4)
6 (a) silly (idea) (*n*) (para 4)
7 to measure (*v*) (para 6)
8 a desire to do something you should not (*n*) (para 7)

b Complete the sentences using words or phrases from Ex. 4a.
1 We _____ on the long, difficult journey.
2 I'm _____ to speak to Phyllis before she leaves.
3 Try to _____ the views while you are here. We might never come back.
4 It was hard to _____ his reaction to the new ideas.
5 There has been a strong _____ to the changes.

How to ... | sound vague

5 a Add one word to each sentence to complete the vague expressions.
1 She's more or _____ finished redecorating.
2 We go camping from _____ to time.
3 I only ever see them once in a blue _____ .
4 I've got a few _____ and pieces to finish off.
5 We work mainly with textiles and _____ kind of thing.
6 We'll be arriving at _____ five-ish.
7 We were sort _____ expecting to hear from you.
8 I was kind _____ hoping you could help.

b **4.2** Listen and check your answers.

> **TAPESCRIPT**
> 1 She's more or less finished redecorating.
> 2 We go camping from time to time.
> 3 I only ever see them once in a blue moon.
> 4 I've got a few bits and pieces to finish off.
> 5 We work mainly with textiles and that kind of thing.
> 6 We'll be arriving at about five-ish.
> 7 We were sort of expecting to hear from you.
> 8 I was kind of hoping you could help.

4.3

Vocabulary | special abilities

1. Complete the sentences by putting the letters in brackets in the correct order.
   1. There is a lot of pressure, and the job is very _____ . (niegmdand)
   2. She is a naturally _____ piano player. (fitegd)
   3. The youngsters in the area are hooligans in the _____ . (kanimg)
   4. Mozart was a musical _____ . (dipogry)
   5. As a film star, he was the subject of much _____ from his fans. (donulatai)
   6. Staff members are trained by their _____ . (srepe)
   7. People with severe disabilities used to be considered _____ . (karsef)

Reading

2. Read the text and make a list of Kishan's interests and achievements.

Nine-year-old calls the shots

(1) The director is barking orders from the edit suite as he cuts a shot featuring Jackie Shroff, a leading Indian film star. It could be an everyday scene of Bollywood folk making their movies – except the director is a nine-year-old boy.

(2) Master Kishan, as he is known, has already been in twenty-four films and appeared in more than 1000 episodes of a popular television soap opera. He is now fulfilling another dream: becoming the youngest director not just in India, but in the world. 'I am different from other children, because this is the age for children to play,' admitted Kishan, sitting in his director's seat, his feet not quite touching the floor. 'I like playing, but not as much as other children. I don't know if the film will be successful, I hope it will be. I have a good feeling about it.'

(3) Dressed in a black corduroy shirt and dark jeans, he looked like any other affluent middle-class Indian child. Later, at a local café, he ordered coffee and mysore pak, a buttery sweet pudding, while fielding approaches from admiring fans.

(4) Kishan, whose favourite actors are Arnold Schwarzenegger and Amithabh Bachchan, a Bollywood superstar, began his acting career aged four after his friends urged his parents to send him for an audition. He was given a part in *Goddess of the Village*, a fantasy adventure, before landing a leading role in *Papa Pandu*, a daily Bangalore soap. He wrote a hit song for a film at the age of six, and has sung on others.

(5) Kishan's father, Shri Kanth, a tax official, said his son had been obsessed with cameras since he was a toddler. 'We noticed that when the camera was on him his behaviour would improve,' he said. 'After he started working on the soap, the staff would complain that he asked too many questions about this shot and that shot.'

(6) Kishan's transition to director began after he talked to children selling newspapers beside a busy road in Bangalore. When he asked them why they were not at school, some replied that they were orphans, others that they would be beaten if they went home without any money. Kishan was so moved that he wrote a short story about his encounter. 'I want them to go to school, and I hope the film encourages them to want to go,' he said.

(7) With the help of local journalists, he turned his story into a screenplay, *C/o Footpath*, about a Bangalore boy drugged by a woman who uses him as a prop to beg on the streets.

(8) Ironically, Kishan's commitments mean that he has attended school for only ten days a month during filming. His secretary collects school notes to help him keep up. Kishan nevertheless shows little sign of missing classes. He speaks good English and Kanada, the local language, and understands Hindi and Tamil.

(9) Shri Kanth, however, worries that his son is missing childhood and recently invited his friends to bring their children on a beach holiday so that Kishan could play. He was surprised to see him building row after row of sand castles. 'When I asked him why he was building them in rows, he held his hands up to make a frame and said it was to give the shot depth,' he said. A child psychologist friend has reassured him his son is fine.

32

4.3

3 Read the text again and answer the questions.
1 What makes Kishan different from other children his age?
2 How did Kishan become involved in acting?
3 What triggered Kishan's move towards becoming a director?
4 What inspired Kishan's short story?
5 What does he hope to achieve through the film?
6 How does Kishan keep up with his school work?
7 Why does his father worry?

4 a Find words or expressions in the text that mean:
1 shouting instructions (para 1) (v) _____
2 wealthy (adj) (para 3) _____
3 encouraged (para 4) (v) _____
4 think about something all the time (para 5) (v) _____
5 be hit many times (v) (para 6) _____
6 feel a strong emotion (sad/sympathetic) (para 6) (adj) _____
7 a meeting (para 6) (n) _____
8 something you use to help achieve a special effect (theatrical) (para 7) (n) _____
9 not fall behind (with work/study) (para 8) (v) _____
10 make someone feel calmer/less worried (para 9) (v) _____

b Underline words and phrases in the text related to films or the media.

Grammar | inversion

5 Choose the correct alternative.
1 No sooner *we had heard/had we heard* the news than the police rang to tell us what had happened.
2 *Not only did she/Not only she did* break the rules, but she also lied about her behaviour.
3 Only when *everyone has arrived/has everyone arrived* can we begin the discussions.
4 Rarely *have I been/I have been* so upset about something.
5 *Not since I went/Since I didn't go* to university have I made so many new friends.
6 No way *I am going/am I going* to pay for their mistake!
7 *Only if/If only* we work day and night will we get the job finished on time.
8 No longer *you do need to/do you need to* stand in long queues at airports. You can check in yourself!
9 Only after she had left *did I/I did* realise what had happened.
10 Not only *the service is great/is the service great*, but it's the cheapest hotel in the area.

6 Complete the sentences with a suitable word or phrase.
1 _____ could be more exotic to explore than these picturesque islands.
2 _____ recently have we begun to understand how the disease spreads.
3 Not _____ the organiser phoned me did I find out about the meeting.
4 No _____ had the plane taken off than they had to make an emergency landing.
5 _____ for one minute did I think I would win the competition.
6 _____ will you find such fantastic examples of the style.
7 Never _____ have we achieved such great sales.
8 _____ when she began to sing did we realise she had a special talent.
9 _____ if you have your bags checked will you be allowed through the entrance.
10 _____ again will I ride on an elephant!

Review and consolidation unit 4

Vocabulary

1 Choose the correct words to complete the sentences.

1. One of the problems is that _____ are over-used nowadays, which creates resistance.
   A antibiotics   B viruses   C skin tissue
2. In the future people will have _____ in our bodies with details of medical records.
   A missions   B microchips   C microscopes
3. _____ have developed a virus which can penetrate the firewall.
   A Organs   B Genes   C Hackers
4. Almost anything is possible with genetic _____.
   A cloning   B engineering   C analyses
5. The rocket was launched into _____.
   A orbit   B mission   C shuttle

Future probability

2 Put the words in the correct order to make sentences.

1. winning the are series against odds them the.
   _____.
2. the we're flight to her on bound see.
   _____.
3. the later it are will chances that rain.
   _____.
4. it we everything time doubtful will that is finish today have to.
   _____.
5. competition is that there a beat distinct we'll the possibility.
   _____.
6. promotion he'll likelihood is every get there that the.
   _____.
7. that idea to well excellent prove may be an.
   _____.
8. there could catch a chance is train that we slim the earlier.
   _____.

Vocabulary

3 Complete the crossword with the missing words.

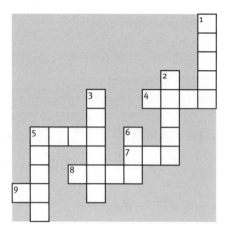

Across
4. I can't make it tomorrow. I'm a bit _____ up.
5. We've had to _____ off the trip because we are just too busy.
7. We were both at a loose _____, so we went out together.
8. Why don't you sit down and put your _____ up?
9. I was wondering what you were _____ to at the weekend.

Down
1. Do you know if the plans are going _____?
2. Have you got anything _____ up for tonight?
3. We were going to Greece for a holiday, but it has all _____ through.
5. I'll let you know if anything _____ up.
6. There's an office party that night and I can't _____ out of it.

Future tenses review

4 Complete the sentences using the correct form of the verbs in brackets. There may be more than one possibility.

1. That's fine. I _____ you next week to confirm the details. (call)
2. We _____ all the work by February. (finish)
3. OK, the taxi _____ to collect us in half an hour. (come)
4. I've got no idea what I _____ next year. (do)
5. Is Anna feeling OK? She looks like she _____ sick. (be)
6. Let me help you. I _____ this pile and you deal with the rest. (take)
7. I have to leave at five o'clock. I _____ Michael to discuss finances. (meet)
8. The traffic is awful. I'm afraid I _____ late. (be)
9. It was really good to see you. Hopefully, I _____ you again soon. (see)
10. I'm stuck at work and I don't know when I _____ home. (get)

34

How to ... | sound vague

5 Complete the mini-dialogues.

1. A: How often to you manage to see your grandmother?
   B: From _____ to time.
2. A: Send me a postcard next time you go.
   B: I would, but we only go there _____ in a blue moon.
3. A: What are you doing later?
   B: Oh, just _____ and pieces.
4. A: How long do you think the meeting will last?
   B: More or _____ all day.
5. A: Shall we get started early?
   B: OK. Shall we say about six _____ ?
6. A: What does your new job involve?
   B: There is a lot of talking to clients and that _____ of thing.
7. A: Let's split the bill.
   B: Actually, I was _____ of hoping you might offer to pay.
8. A: What time shall we meet?
   B: About eight or _____ .

Inversion

6 There are mistakes in seven of the sentences. Tick (✓) the correct sentences and correct the others.

1. Not only they apologised for the inconvenience, but they have refunded the money!
2. No sooner do you ask her to do a job than she has done it.
3. Only after did I repeatedly ask them, did I manage to get a response.
4. Not since 2005 there has been such a hot summer.
5. Rarely do you find someone with such great talent.
6. Never before we have been able to photograph these small creatures in such detail.
7. Only if we keep looking we will ever find the solution.
8. No way am I going to dress up as Superman!
9. Not for one minute did I thought they really meant what they said.
10. Nowhere it does say that we aren't allowed to use this room.

Vocabulary

7 Complete the sentences with a suitable word.

1. The police don't seem to be able maintain law and _____ .
2. _____ and large, we don't come across too many problems of this type.
3. We'll have to work it out by _____ and error.
4. It's difficult to keep up with all the new rules and _____ .
5. He's always complaining of _____ and pains.
6. Don't worry. It's a _____ and tested formula.
7. The lecturer bombarded us with _____ and figures about the economy.
8. I've got no idea where he could be. He's always out and _____ .
9. We need to sort this matter out _____ and for all.
10. We are all _____ and waiting.
11. I only see my aunt now and _____ .
12. I'm sick and _____ of clearing up everyone else's mess.
13. I'm not sure how long it's going to take. First, I need to sort out some bits and _____ in the office.
14. I get terrible headaches from time to _____ .
15. I think we have more or _____ finished, unless anyone else has something to add.

5.1 Fortunes

Vocabulary | finance

1 Put the letters in brackets in the correct order. Then use the words to complete the sentences.

1. He came into a small _____ when his father died. (netourf)
2. It is common practice to _____ in the shops to bring the price down. (galgeh)
3. These young bankers make their fortunes betting on changes in the _____ market. (ctoks)
4. Let me buy everyone a drink. I got a _____ today! (sier)
5. The business is trying to attract _____ families. (ghih-monice)
6. Her ideas are unique, so her work is absolutely _____. (crisepels)
7. It doesn't affect our salary as we're paid on _____. (smocsimino)
8. They have done really well considering their last business went _____. (knaptrub)

2 Choose the correct alternative.

1. Murray kept his *cold/cool/heat* throughout the difficult match.
2. Credit card *criminal/fake/fraud* is on the increase.
3. Some children have a very limited attention *space/span/time*.
4. It's important to get some hands-on work *experience/experts/experienced* before leaving university.
5. We've asked the bank for some start-up *lends/loan/funds*.
6. The girl who catches the bridal *bouquet/veil/dress* will be the next to marry.
7. It's unusual for a new business to make a *proof/profit/living* in the first year.
8. There is a glimmer of *chance/possible/hope* because we've found someone to lend us the money.

Grammar | emphasis

3 Rewrite the sentences to increase the emphasis. Use the words in brackets.

The average house price in the UK is now £170,000 making it increasingly difficult for young people to buy a home. (own)

The average house price in the UK is £170,000 making it increasingly difficult for young people to buy their own home.

1. The fact that 1 in 10 children in the UK are suffering from a mental health disorder is worrying. (indeed)
2. Americans are not very interested in soccer. They prefer to watch baseball. (all)
3. It isn't certain that giving aid is the best way to help poorer countries. (means)
4. Kandinsky abandoned his law studies in order to train as an artist in Munich. (even)
5. The most popular soap opera in South American history, *I Am Betty The Ugly*, was so successful because the woman who played Betty was incredibly beautiful. (reason)
6. Marco Diacono planted the UK's first ever olive grove in 2006. He hoped that global warming would help the trees to survive. (person)
7. We went to the Pantanal, in Brazil, to enjoy the wildlife, but I got a shock when I found an eight-foot-long caiman alligator outside my tent. (did)
8. I would suggest you stay along the coast from Amalfi. (place)

4 Match the sentence halves.

1. It was important that the brothers had a good relationship, as they were ☐
2. They decided to buy their uncle ☐
3. You need to strike the ☐
4. It's time he rolled up his ☐
5. They hired a consultant to ☐
6. They kept their business and private affairs separate in order not to ☐
7. I have come from a marketing ☐
8. It will be up to the new manager to execute the ☐

a. sleeves and got on with what he has to do.
b. crunch the numbers.
c. fifty-fifty partners in the business.
d. jeopardise their friendship.
e. right balance between working hard and enjoying yourself.
f. strategy we decide on.
g. out of his share of the company.
h. background.

Reading and Listening

5 🔊 **5.1** Read and listen to the text. Answer the questions.

1. What memories does the writer have of her father at home?
2. Why do you think she particularly remembers the sound of the electronic gates?
3. What would happen to her mother when they arrived at the prison?
4. How did the young girl react to this?
5. How was she able to make physical contact with her father during the visits?
6. What things did she notice about him during the trips?

Child of the incarcerated

(1) I have only a small child's handful of memories of life with my father. At home after my tap dancing debut at four; a heated argument between him and my mother around the same time; and mostly and most vividly, the trips to visit him once he was serving time in Greenhaven State Penitentiary in Stormville, New York.

(2) I remember the long ride to get there. Along the way was an Indian gift shop with a teepee outside. We stopped there once, on our way home, to look at moccasins and coin purses. When we arrived at the prison, there was a series of electronic gates to pass through, papers to show. My mother was fingerprinted. They looked through her purse and patted her body down. We didn't talk while this went on. I was good at reading signals. This was serious stuff. I felt hot and sad.

(3) The visiting room was a big, bright white and steel institutional space. Guards sat at a desk, at one end of the room, taking in the exchanges between inmates and guests. We chose seats on opposite sides of a giant stainless-steel counter, accessible to him from the inside, through a barred electronic door. From counter surface to floor was solid wall, from counter to ceiling a chain link fence with one-inch square openings, large enough to fit your fingers through, for a touch, or your pursed lips, for a kiss. We talked in low murmured tones on our visits, for privacy. Sometimes the room would be full and there'd be a buzz like a hive. We tried not to sit close to anyone else. He wore greenish-gray pants and a matching shirt with buttons. He always smiled and sauntered over. He was so handsome and fit and tall. I don't remember what we talked about, or how often I went to see him. The visits were a chance to make contact – to hear his voice, to see the color of his skin, his smile, the shape of his fingernails. To imprint his stride on my memory. To notice things I probably wouldn't if I saw him every day.

6 Find words or phrases in the text that mean, or suggest:

1. the first time she danced this style (*n*) (para 1) _____
2. an angry discussion (*n*) (para 1) _____
3. an Indian tent (*n*) (para 2) _____
4. Indian shoes (*n*) (para 2) _____
5. the noise the electronic prison door made (*n*) (para 2) _____
6. prisoners (*n*) (para 3) _____
7. a large metal surface (*n*) (para 3) _____
8. the noise of bees (*n*) (para 3) _____
9. the place where bees live (*n*) (para 3) _____
10. walked casually (*v*) (para 3) _____

5.2

Vocabulary

1 Write in the missing word in each sentence.

1. The manager took advantage the situation and increased his own salary.
2. The army have volunteered help move people out of the disaster area.
3. The furniture has all been reduced so now you can get nearly fifty percent the original price.
4. Unfortunately, the footballer gave his wife of attorney, and she spent all the money.
5. The local farmers invested in the water company, but never saw a of the profit that was made.
6. The residents have been pestering the government change the law.
7. He was a media millionaire, but after the scandal he bankruptcy.
8. The driver of the train hasn't been able to work since the accident, so he lives off a disability from the government.

Grammar | conditionals

2 Complete the sentences with the correct form of the verbs in brackets.

1. If I _____ my car here, I _____ you a lift. (have) (offer)
2. I _____ some coffee if everyone _____ eating. (make) (finish)
3. If it _____ for Jamie, we _____ for ages. (not be) (wait)
4. If you _____ carefully to what I said, this _____ ! (listen) (not happen)
5. Provided that she _____ all the right injections, she _____ fine. (have) (be)
6. If only they _____ us ten minutes earlier, we _____ the order. (ring) (cancel)
7. Unless Graham _____ his strategy, the business _____ bankrupt. (change) (go)
8. Should you happen _____ in Oxford, you _____ and stay. (be) (come)
9. Supposing they _____ her the job, would she _____ it? (offer) (accept)
10. I _____ how much it costs, so long as the job _____ by Sunday. (not mind) (finish)

3 Complete the first half of the sentences with a suitable word. Then <u>underline</u> the correct second halves.

1. _____ that the team keep playing as they are at the moment,
   we had a good chance of winning the cup.
   we have a good chance of winning the cup.
2. Should you _____ to see Martin on your travels,
   could you tell him I've been trying to contact him?
   you could have told him I'd been trying to contact him.
3. If it _____ been for Kate telling us,
   we never realised what they were planning.
   we never would have realised what they were planning.
4. If you _____ like to see the rest of the house,
   I could have left the key and you could show yourself around.
   I can leave you the key and you can show yourself around.
5. If _____ we hadn't bought the tickets already,
   then we could change our plans.
   then we changed our plans.
6. As _____ as Sheila still works there,
   she should be able to give you all the information you need.
   she could be able to give you all the information you need.

Vocabulary | charity

4 Complete the text using words from the box.

lavishly donating deal inspired vision
generosity impact admirable Foundation
charity dedicate fortune mission

Warren Buffet, the world's greatest stock market investor, announced he was giving away most of his $24 billion (1) _____ . The world's second richest man is (2) _____ the money to the Bill and Melinda Gates (3) _____ , whose (4) _____ is to tackle AIDS and global poverty. This is (5) _____ on an industrial scale. The (6) _____ of these two men will now far outstrip the contribution of most aid organisations to Africa. The knock-on effect could have an equally significant (7) _____ : if important role-models (8) _____ a great (9) _____ of their wealth to helping the poor and the sick, then perhaps others might be (10) _____ to give away money rather than simply spend (11) _____ on themselves and their families. Two hundred years ago, William Blake argued that charity, however (12) _____ on an individual level, is wrong because it delays reform and perpetuates economic injustice. Doubtless many still agree with that view. But the sheer scale of the Gates–Buffett 'mega-merger', their joint (13) _____ for a way towards a better future, is surely bad news for critics of the market system.

Instant millionaires need help

1 The high-tech world is making thousands of very young people very rich, but according to psychologists it is also creating a new illness — sudden wealth syndrome.

2 Some seek help because they are too rich and cannot handle their wealth, others because they crave more money or feel guilty. Dr Stephen Goldbart, a psychologist, runs the Money, Meaning & Choices Institute near Silicon Valley, where sixty-four new millionaires are reportedly created every day. Most of them are people in their twenties and thirties who find themselves suddenly rich, a group Dr Goldbart calls the 'Siliconaires'.

3 He noticed a change about ten years ago when people from middle-class backgrounds started coming into large sums of money. With the dot.com trend of recent years, his client numbers have steadily increased. In April, Merrill Lynch reported that the number of millionaires in the United States and Canada has risen almost forty percent since 1997 to 2.5 million.

4 Becoming unexpectedly rich has its drawbacks, Dr Goldbart says, and there should be some amount of sympathy for those who cannot handle sudden wealth. 'It can ruin their lives, rip their families apart and lead them on a path of destructive behaviour,' he says. 'Money does not always bring peace and fulfilment. They lose balance. Instead of money solving all their problems it often brings guilt, stress and confusion.'

5 People who are used to working 80 to 100 hours a week on their fledgling enterprise suddenly find they no longer need to work and are able to retire at the age of thirty. However, the newfound leisure puts them into a premature, mid-life crisis. Some experience panic attacks, severe depression and insomnia, Dr Goldbart says. Others withdraw from society or go on maniacal shopping sprees.

6 Some newly rich feel guilty about having so much money and feel they are not entitled to it, or that they do not deserve it. Others become paranoid, thinking they will be exploited because of their wealth, or they become obsessed with making even more money. People most affected are the 'new rich', for whom wealth was not part of their upbringing and who expected to spend their lives working. Anxiety and depression can also come from 'ticker shock' as they watch the vagaries in the stock market, particularly a plunge when they have not exercised their stock options.

7 Part of Dr Goldbart's cure for the unhappy rich is to get them involved in the community and not just writing cheques to charities. British Columbia's Rory Holland, executive vice-president of Itemus, made his millions when the company he was involved in for eight years was sold for US$103-million in 1998. He now devotes much of his time to four non-profit groups, serves on their boards and helps raise money.

8 Dr Goldbart believes he is the only psychologist, along with family counsellor Joan DiFuria, providing therapy for the rich, and would like to see more colleagues provide the service. 'These people [the rich] are sensitive to how people feel and are reluctant to use our kind of service,' he says. 'But we help them regain the balance they've lost.'

Reading

5 Read the article quickly. What is the significance of these numbers?

1 64
2 30s
3 10
4 2.5 million
5 80–100
6 30
7 US$103 million

6 Read the article again. Answer the questions.

1 What has caused the increase in the number of millionaires?
2 What feelings can someone who comes into sudden wealth experience? How can these feelings affect them?
3 Who might be particularly affected?
4 What might be the cause of these feelings?
5 What does Dr Goldbart suggest as a cure?
6 How does Dr Goldbart feel the public should treat sudden millionaires?

7 Complete the sentences with words or phrases from the text.

1 I've got so much work on at the moment, I just can't _____ it. (para 2)
2 I've given up caffeine, but I still _____ coffee first thing in the morning. (para 2)
3 For me, the advantages outweigh the _____ when you're living in a city like London. (para 4)
4 The effect of the earthquake was literally to _____ the whole community. (para 4)
5 The plans aren't very advanced yet. It's just a _____ idea. (para 5)
6 He's given up his job, taken up jogging and started dancing classes. I think he's having a _____ . (para 5)
7 She took all the credit for the ideas, even when she is not strictly _____ to. (para 6)
8 My father died when I was young, so we had a rather difficult _____ . (para 6)

5.3

Vocabulary | in the office

1 Complete the crossword with the missing words.

Across

3 One of the best things about working here is the _____ of the location.
5 One of the _____ of the job is this fantastic company car!
6 As a boss, he is very _____ of his staff.
9 The pay is $39,000 a year, which is a good _____ .
11 It's a great job if you have children because of the _____ working hours.
12 The company invests in a private _____ plan on your behalf.
13 We get strange requests from our clients, so some of our tasks can be quite _____ .
14 Most of the workers enjoyed a high degree of job _____ .

Down

1 The offices are modern and spacious, and there are lots of like-minded people, so it's a really good working _____ .
2 We attend conferences and workshops as part of our professional _____ .
4 Glenco is an international company so there are plenty of travel _____ .
7 It's a good job with excellent promotion _____ .
8 The staff received bonuses in recognition of their _____ .
10 I enjoy the _____ of working for myself.

How to … | express priorities

2 **a** Put the words in the correct order to make sentences.

1 to for work is to walk essential to me able the thing be.
   _____
   _____

2 absolutely prospects having promotion vital is good.
   _____
   _____

3 major a flexible isn't having hours priority working.
   _____
   _____

4 job is main priority satisfaction my.
   _____
   _____

5 couldn't supportive without I colleagues do.
   _____
   _____

6 pension really about a not plan I'm having bothered.
   _____
   _____

b [5.2] Listen and check your answers.

TAPESCRIPT

1 The essential thing for me is to be able to walk to work.
2 Having good promotion prospects is absolutely vital.
3 Having flexible working hours isn't a major priority.
4 My main priority is job satisfaction.
5 I couldn't do without supportive colleagues.
6 I'm not really bothered about having a pension plan.

c Listen again. Do 1–3 below.

1 Underline the words that carry the main stress.
2 Circle the syllable that is stressed.
3 Repeat the sentences, copying the rhythm.

40

Grammar | sentence adverbials

3 Rewrite the sentences using the words in CAPITALS.

As far as I can see, there is nothing we can do to stop the plans going ahead. SEEMINGLY

There is seemingly nothing we can do to stop the plans going ahead.

1 You may be surprised to hear that sales figures were up on last year. BELIEVE

2 Everyone says that the company is losing a lot of money. APPARENTLY

3 For the most part the management have a good relationship with the rest of the staff. BROADLY

4 In my opinion, the conclusions of the report are wrong. FUNDAMENTALLY

5 I'd like to say no to the extra work but I need the money. HAND

6 What you say is true, but only in part. POINT

7 I travel a lot for my job. On the whole I enjoy it although it can be exhausting. LARGE

8 Looking back, we should probably have approached them earlier. WITH

9 Unexpectedly, the results of the survey indicate that there could be a good market for the new product. ENOUGH

Listening

4 a 5.3 Cover the tapescript. Listen to the interview and answer the questions.

1 What is Rachel Stanmore's job?
2 What kind of company is MediaCom?

b Listen again and make notes about:
- Creative ideas and strange food
- Inspiring the workers
- Number of employees/average age of workers
- Schemes and new ideas

Vocabulary | expressing quantity

5 Complete the tapescript using words from the box.

> little   deal   few   plenty   vast
> most   awful   not   many

TAPESCRIPT

I: Crocodile curry and cheesy worms may not be everybody's idea of snack food, but MediaCom, rated number twenty-eight in the Sunday Times listing of 'Top 100 companies to work for', wants to encourage a creative and original take on the world. So they offer chocolate ants to their workers at break times and have (1) _____ of other interesting ideas, too. With us this morning is Rachel Stanmore, a business expert who has spent some time in this innovative media company. And she's here to tell us more about it. Good morning, Rachel.

R: Good morning.

I: Now I'm (2) _____ much of an expert in these things, so what is it, Rachel, that the company's trying to achieve with these rather strange ideas?

R: Um... well, the philosophy is that the company will do better if the workers are inspired. They don't want people coming to work thinking: 'Oh – it's just another day at the office.' So they've hired a 'Director of Freshness'. Er... it's her responsibility to make the workplace more inspiring, so she spends an (3) _____ lot of time thinking up ideas such as working in the park on a sunny day, or having magicians in the office. They want people to be on tenterhooks, wondering what's going to happen next, hence the assaults on their senses, like crocodile curry for lunch, or foot spas in the afternoon.

I: Can you tell us a (4) _____ bit more about the company?

R: Um... sure. It's the UK's largest billing media agency, with 389 employees based in London and Edinburgh. The (5) _____ majority of the workers are young professionals, under thirty-five, who may be earning a great (6) _____ of money, but more importantly they like to feel appreciated, and constantly motivated. For the (7) _____ part they are fully behind the business, with as (8) _____ as eight out of ten of the staff feeling excited about where the company's going. And that's because they have control – they know what it's like to run things. Quite a (9) _____ of them have had their own ideas brought into operation. Last year, for example, there was a scheme called: 'If I ran the company', and as a result a company bar was introduced, which provides free breakfasts in the morning, is also open until 11.30 at night, and has the boss working behind it.

I: Free breakfasts – now that's a better idea, although it's not chocolate ants, I hope! And what about other incentives? What other kinds of incentive are there?

Review and consolidation unit 5

Vocabulary

1 Match the sentence halves.
1 She hasn't had to worry about money since they sold the business and she came ☐
2 We are paid a fixed salary, plus a ten percent commission ☐
3 He managed to bring the price down by ☐
4 His internet business went ☐
5 It was a great business idea. Now she is waiting to get the ☐
6 If you know what you are doing, there is plenty of money ☐
7 The house is filled with priceless ☐
8 I'm not sure how they manage to make a ☐
9 The bank manager left them without a glimmer ☐
10 Ana is helping in the office to gain some work ☐

a start-up funds.
b bankrupt a few years ago.
c living at all.
d antiques.
e on any sales we agree.
f of hope.
g experience.
h to be made on the stock market.
i into a fortune.
j haggling with the owner.

Conditional sentences

2 Complete each sentence by adding a word from the box.

> don't   would   you   as   only   were   for

1 If it hadn't been the weather, we would have had a wonderful holiday.
2 You can use my phone provided that you speak for too long.
3 If I had listened to her advice!
4 Should happen to be in Rome, you should call my sister.
5 Supposing we to call the police, that might help.
6 If you let us know as soon as the parcel arrives.
7 As long he lives in that house, I'm not going back there.

Emphasis

3 Choose the correct words to complete the sentences.
1 The main reason _____ is that I didn't enjoy the atmosphere.
   A why leaving
   B why I left
   C for I left
2 Whatever _____ when she told us there was no alternative?
   A she did mean
   B she means
   C did she mean
3 I _____ him take the money.
   A actually saw
   B saw actually
   C actual saw
4 They were so relieved to finally buy _____ house.
   A their own
   B on their own
   C own their
5 The journey was _____ .
   A by means no easy
   B by no means easy
   C no means by easy
6 _____ impresses me about them is that they are so efficient.
   A The most thing that
   B The thing that most
   C Most the thing that
7 The main ideas are _____ .
   A very indeed interesting
   B interesting very indeed
   C very interesting indeed
8 It's incredible! He's not _____ .
   A interested all at football
   B interested in football all at
   C interested in football at all

Vocabulary

4 Use the clues to complete the crossword.

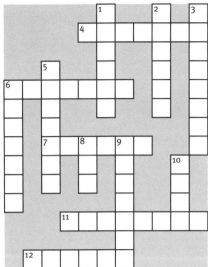

Across
4 Their _____ was to help the homeless.
6 They spend a _____ on childcare so that they can both go to work.
7 The changes have definitely had a major _____ .
11 Take a look at their _____ illustrated catalogue.
12 Don't eat any more. You're just being _____ .

Down
1 She enjoys _____ money to a good cause.
2 Our _____ is to expand the business over the next five years.
3 Her work has _____ others to join the profession.
5 A wage of £100 a week is hardly enough to _____ for a growing family.
6 The organisation was _____ in the mid-1990s.
8 He _____ most of the money into a high-interest bank account.
9 I give all my old clothes to _____ .
10 The government has spent a great _____ of money on renovating the old buildings.

5 Complete the sentences using the correct form of the words in CAPITALS.
1 My work gives me a lot of job _____ . SATISFY
2 Luckily, my boss is very _____ . SUPPORT
3 The pay isn't very good initially, but there are good _____ prospects. PROMOTE
4 Working to deadlines can be quite _____ . CHALLENGE
5 The company helps with your personal and professional _____ . DEVELOP
6 My role was changed in _____ of my abilities. RECOGNISE
7 Having worked nights for so long, it is great to have such _____ working hours. FLEX
8 One of the benefits of the apartment is the _____ of its location. CONVENIENT

6 Cross out (✗) the alternatives which are NOT possible, or have a different meaning.
1 We try to support each other, and _____ it seems to work.
   A by and large   B however   C broadly speaking
2 Transcil always deal with the problem quickly. _____ , they do charge a lot for their services.
   A Essentially   B On the other hand
   C However
3 We cut our prices by nearly fifty percent and _____ we managed to increase our profits.
   A believe it or not   B surprisingly enough   C with hindsight
4 They moved the factory to China to cut costs. _____ it was the right decision.
   A With hindsight   B Looking back
   C However
5 The business is _____ a technical marketing company.
   A essentially   B looking back
   C fundamentally
6 She is working for herself, and _____ doing very well.
   A on the other hand   B apparently
   C seemingly

Idioms | money

7 Write in the missing word in each sentence.
1 He sold his business for $14 million. He's a fortune.
2 As a student I lived the money I earned from waitressing jobs.
3 Since my husband lost his job, we're not very well financially.
4 I have spent this month's salary, so now I completely broke.
5 You don't need to pay for everything. Let's split bill.
6 You should treat to something special at least once a month.
7 It's a beautiful dress, and the best thing about it is that it was dirt.
8 Let's splash on a meal in an expensive restaurant.
9 I shouldn't worry about paying back the money. She's rolling it.
10 My wage brings us more than enough to get on.
11 I'm glad you like the carpet. It cost me an and a leg.
12 It's very expensive to buy on my own, but perhaps we could go.

43

6.1 Power

Listening

1 a 🔊 6.1 Cover the tapescript. Listen to the news story and answer the questions.

1. What is the purpose of the international vote?
2. What happened to the original seven wonders?

b Listen again and take notes under the headings.

> The voting process _____
>
> _____
>
> Bernard Weber _____
>
> _____
>
> Criticisms of the new list _____
>
> _____

c Choose the best definition. Look at the tapescript to help you.

1. spawn (v)
   A take photos using advanced technology
   B inspire others to copy something, or produce/generate something
2. stuffy (adj)
   A dull and too formal/not very lively
   B the most famous
3. contender (n)
   A a type of building found in ancient cities
   B person or thing taking part in a competition
4. definitive (adj)
   A final/complete/able to serve as a perfect example
   B long-lasting
5. weed out (p.v.)
   A remove the worst/weakest from a list or group
   B put forward an argument for the one you think is the best
6. shortlist (n)
   A winner, following a long discussion
   B group of the best candidates for final consideration (in a competition)
7. ransack (v)
   A change the structure of a building by adding parts
   B search violently in order to steal something

TAPESCRIPT

They have sheltered kings, protected nations from invaders, inspired the world's greatest artists and spawned a million postcards. Now the world's most glorified buildings are to be officially recognised, not by the United Nations or a stuffy bunch of architects, but by the common man and woman, or at least those with Internet access.

Millions of people are taking part in an international vote to pick seven new wonders of the world. The contenders include the Statue of Liberty, Petra in Jordan, the Colosseum, the Acropolis, and the statue of Christ the Redeemer in Rio de Janeiro. The campaign, via the modern wonder of the Internet, was launched by adventurer, filmmaker and entrepreneur Bernard Weber, who says he wants to create a definitive list, chosen in a democratic fashion.

After an initial weeding out process, twenty-one wonders remain, the final seven of which will be determined by the number of votes cast in their favour on www.new7wonders.com. The winning sites will be filmed by Mr Weber. However, not everyone is happy with the shortlist. The absence of technology disappointed Stuart Leslie, a professor at Johns Hopkins University. He claims that the Internet should be on the list simply because it allows us to access all the other wonders. Mr Leslie's list would also include inventions such as the hydrogen bomb and nylon.

Of the old seven wonders, only one still exists: the Great Pyramid of Giza. The others have been destroyed over the years by a combination of earthquakes, fire, and greed, as invaders ransacked palaces and temples. Though Weber admits he has no idea how long the new seven wonders will last, he's having a lot of fun naming them.

Pronunciation | speed and rhythm in connected speech

2 a Listen to the recording again. Read aloud at the same time.

b Repeat until you can follow the speed and rhythm on the recording.

44

Grammar | articles

3 Choose *a*, *an*, *the* or no article (–).

Easter Island

Easter Island is (1) *a/an/the/–* remote place 2200 miles off (2) *a/an/the/–* coast of Chile. It has barely 4000 inhabitants, one airport and some simple accommodation for tourists. It used to be full of (3) *a/an/the/–* lush trees but they died centuries ago. Yet Easter Island is world famous. There are few more powerful and mysterious sights than (4) *a/an/the/–* island's magnificent statues, called moai, rising up out of the barren landscape thirteen feet high and weighing fourteen tons.

These huge stone heads were carved from (5) *a/an/the/–* volcanic rock between four and nine hundred years ago. With their elongated faces and deep-set eyes, they are (6) *a/an/the/–* incredibly haunting sight, and there are 887 of them. But what was their purpose?

(7) *A/An/The/–* archaeologists suggest that (8) *a/an/the/–* statues were symbols of religious and political power, or perhaps depictions of the spirits of early ancestors. There are other mysteries surrounding (9) *a/an/the/–* moai. They were not built where they are found, so how were they transported? What's more, the majority of the moai have been knocked down and now lie on their faces or in (10) *a/an/the/–* pieces. Why? We will probably never know.

How to ... | describe an important building/structure

4 Complete the sentences by adding or cutting one word. One sentence is correct.

1. The Taj Mahal is probably most famous building in India.
2. The Ice Hotel, Quebec, is entirely made up from ice.
3. Maya Ying Lin designed a famous wall in Washington DC as memorial for the soldiers who died in Vietnam.
4. The Arc de Triomphe, Paris, was built honour of Napoleon's military conquests.
5. Covering an area of a million square feet, Paris's Pompidou Centre is one of Europe's greatest cultural centres.
6. The Great Wall of China is around 4000 miles long and 7.5 metres up high.
7. The Mayan pyramids may have been used for to house the bodies of kings.
8. Turkey's greatest church, the Hagia Sophia, is said to have built in just five years.

Writing

5 Read the notes about two pieces of architecture that didn't go to plan. Choose one and write a short essay about it. Use phrases from page 78 of the Students' Book to help you.

Leaning Tower of Pisa
- a bell tower, next to Pisa Cathedral, Pisa, Italy
- started 1173, completed 1372 (wars prevented completion)
- architect: Pisano and di Simone + others??
- problem: started early on, during construction
- 1990-2001 closed for repairs and reconstruction. Now stable for next 300 years.

Millennium Bridge
- footbridge across the River Thames, London, UK
- started 1999, opened June 10th 2000
- architect: Arup, Foster and Partners + sculptor Sir Anthony Caro
- problem: bridge swayed (nickname The Wobbly Bridge!) when people walked on it
- June 12th 2000 bridge closed to stabilise
- February 22nd 2002 re-opened. No sway!

6.2

Reading

1 a Read the article quickly and choose the best sub-heading.
1. How technology is changing the way our students learn
2. Email etiquette at university
3. How professors and students keep in touch

Student power -

(1) One student skipped class and then sent the professor an email message asking for copies of the teaching notes. Another didn't like her grade and sent a petulant message to the professor. Another explained that she was late for a Monday class because she was recovering from a party. One professor received a message from a student, saying, 'I'm not sure how to shop for school supplies. Should I buy a binder or a subject notebook? Would you let me know your recommendations?' At colleges and universities, email has made professors more approachable, but many say it has made them too accessible. They say that students seem to view them as available round the clock, sending a steady stream of email messages – from ten a week to ten after every class – that are too informal or simply inappropriate. Michael J. Kessler, a lecturer at Georgetown University, says 'The tone that they take in an email is pretty astounding. "I need to know this and you need to tell me right now." It's a fine balance to accommodate what they need and at the same time maintain a level of legitimacy as an instructor. We are authorised to make demands on them, and not the other way round.'

(2) Professor Patricia Ewick of Clark University, Massachusetts, said ten students emailed her drafts of their papers days before they were due, seeking comments. Ewick says, 'It's all different levels of presumption. One is that I'll be able to drop everything and read 250 pages two days before I'm going to get fifty of these.' Robert B. Ahdieh, associate professor of law, said he had received emails with messages such as 'you're covering the material too fast' or 'I don't think we're using the reading as much as we could in class' or 'I think it would be helpful if you would summarise what we've covered at the end of class in case we missed anything.' While once professors expected deference, their expertise seems to have become just another service that students, as consumers, are buying. So students may have no fear of giving offence or imposing on the professor's time. Many professors say they are uncertain how to react to the emails. For example, the professor who was asked about buying the notebook said she debated whether to tell the student that this was not a query that should be directed to her, but worried that 'such a message could be pretty scary' and decided not to respond at all.

(3) Most professors, however, emphasised that instant feedback could be invaluable. One professor said that questions about a lecture or discussion indicated 'a blind spot', that the student obviously didn't understand something. Others have probably hit on the best solution by making rules for email: telling students how quickly the professor would respond, how messages should be drafted and what type of messages they would answer. Meg Worley, an assistant professor of English, tells students that they must say thank you after receiving a professor's response to an email. 'The less powerful person always has to write back,' she said.

b Complete the notes using one word in each space.

In higher education, professors are now more (1) _____ than they used to be because of (2) _____.
The problem: students either write too (3) _____ emails or write emails that are (4) _____ (maybe too informal or stupid).
Kessler says he doesn't like the (5) _____ of the emails he receives.
Ewick thinks that students these days (6) _____ too much, and seem to think their teachers have lots of free (7) _____.
Ahdieh received criticisms of his (8) _____ by email.
A lot of professors aren't (9) _____ how to respond to these emails.
Some professors have solved the problem by making (10) _____ about the class's email use.

c Tick (✓) the sentences that are true according to the article.

1 The professors said that students rarely <u>missed</u> lessons without good reasons. (para 1) ☐
2 Some students write <u>angry</u> emails and behave like little children. (para 1) ☐
3 As a professor, you have to maintain your <u>credibility</u> in front of students. (para 1) ☐
4 One professor asked students to email the first <u>version</u> of their compositions. (para 2) ☐
5 Students' emails show that the traditional <u>humility towards</u> professors isn't as common as it used to be. (para 2) ☐
6 Many professors said that receiving criticisms by email was <u>extremely useful</u> to them. (para 3) ☐
7 Emails about lectures sometimes showed there was <u>an area that the student didn't grasp properly</u>. (para 3) ☐
8 Some professors <u>found a perfect answer to the problem</u> by banning email correspondence. (para 3) ☐

d Find words and expressions in the article that match the <u>underlined</u> words/expressions in Ex. 1c.

Grammar | whatever/whoever/whenever/however

2 Seven of these sentences contain one mistake. Tick (✓) the correct sentences and correct the mistakes in the others.

1 Whoever you are, you have to pay $10 to get in. _____
2 Giles is your driver. Where you want to go, he will take you. _____
3 Whatever we want to do, we have to get permission from the boss. _____
4 How you look at it, whether you are staff or customers, it's a stupid rule. _____
5 Whenever the teacher comes into the room, the students stand up. _____
6 What you said, I didn't hear you because of the music. _____
7 I'll talk to whoever I can in order to get you an interview. _____
8 Who you spoke to, it wasn't the boss, but a criminal impersonator! _____
9 Help me however you can. _____
10 My mum told me I had that mark whenever I was born. _____
11 Wherever I go, that beautiful woman seems to follow. _____
12 How you choose to join, whether online or in person, it is a great deal. _____

3 Choose the correct alternative.

Parent Power

Desperate parents in Gigo, New Zealand, decided to write a manifesto for the children in the town, following a drop in standards of behaviour. 'I'm not sure (1) *why/however* it got so bad, but (2) *whatever/whenever* one of us tried to discipline our kids, they would just swear at us,' says Joe Malonga. (3) '*Whatever/However* we tried to do, it failed. We tried bribing them, punishing them and eventually begging them. Nothing worked.' So, (4) *whenever/when* Malonga suggested drawing up a list of rules, other parents agreed immediately. (5) '*Who/Whoever* thought of a rule had to be backed by seventy percent of the parents. Then we persuaded the kids to sign the document, and posted hundreds of copies around town.' (6) *Where/Wherever* you look – in shops, schools, bus stops – you can see Gigo's Twelve Golden Rules. 'So far it's worked a treat,' says Malonga.

Vocabulary | phrasal verbs

4 Add the correct words to the sentences.

1 How do you manage to keep coming so many great ideas?
   A up to   B over with   C up with
2 The concert will kick a half-hour set by the grunge band, Easy Daze.
   A onto   B off with   C up with
3 This is our new product. We're hoping it will catch in the Far East especially.
   A up   B off   C on
4 Revolutions tend to come because of desperation on a huge scale.
   A through   B on   C about
5 According to fashion guru Leila Wintour, lacy stockings are this winter, and every woman should have a pair.
   A off   B in   C up
6 It can be difficult to keep the news on the island because the post only comes once a month and there's no Internet.
   A up with   B up to   C on with
7 The company decided to home new technology, focussing its attention on digital software.
   A in to   B in on   C up to
8 While hats were fashionable last summer, they seem to be this year.
   A on   B off   C out

6.3

Listening

1 a [6.2] Cover the tapescript. Listen to three people discussing charisma. Mark the statements true (T) or false (F).

1. The men think that people sometimes confuse fame and charisma. ☐
2. The woman doesn't like film stars much. ☐
3. The woman thinks sports people are often charismatic. ☐
4. The woman believes that most politicians have a little bit of charisma. ☐
5. The men are surprised by the woman's opinions. ☐

b Listen again. Complete the sentences from the tapescript with the word(s) you hear.

1. I think most famous people actually have no charisma _____ .
2. Most film stars are short, ugly and boring, and _____ .
3. ... as they open their mouths, out comes a _____ of _____ .
4. ... if it wasn't _____ his achievements in a boxing ring, Ali would just be a _____ .
5. I never knew you were so _____ , Joan.
6. Wow, that's a bit of an _____ .

c Look at the tapescript and check your answers.

Grammar | link words of time and contrast

2 Cross out (✗) the alternative which is NOT possible.

1. The waiter didn't bring the food until midnight, *by which time/at which point/despite* Sarah was starving.
2. *No sooner had I arrived than/I'd hardly arrived when/On arriving*, Don left.
3. *Whilst/When/While* we like pasta, we don't want to eat it every day.
4. He finished the race *despite/even though/although* he felt sick.
5. We can't understand your theory, *much as/in spite/hard as* we try.
6. *On falling asleep/She hardly falls asleep/No sooner does she fall asleep than* she starts snoring.
7. No one goes to bed before 2 a.m. *during the festival/while the festival is going on/as long as the festival is*.
8. *Although/Despite/In spite of* your behaviour, everyone had a good time yesterday.

TAPESCRIPT

Pete: I'm never quite sure if people are really charismatic or if it's just something to do with fame. Being famous kind of makes you automatically charismatic.

Bryn: Like when a film star walks into a restaurant, you mean, and everyone turns and stares and says: 'Oh, what charisma,' but actually it's just that this person's famous.

Pete: Exactly.

Joan: I think most famous people actually have no charisma whatsoever. Most film stars are short, ugly and boring, and self-obsessed, which is just another way of being boring, of course.

Pete: D'you really think so?

Joan: Oh yeah, half of them are tiny. And they have bad skin.

Bryn: Well, sportsmen and women are usually quite impressive, physically.

Joan: Yeah, but then they have nothing to say, do they? They spend their whole life in the gym or beating each other up, so as soon as they open their mouths, out comes a stream of nonsense.

Pete: But don't you think some of them are charismatic? Muhammad Ali or Pelé, people like that.

Joan: No.

Bryn: What do you mean 'no'?!

Joan: Well, if it wasn't for his achievements in a boxing ring, Ali would just be a loudmouth. I don't think that's charismatic at all. Same with all performing artists. They are good at one thing and everyone then assumes that they have some magical, mystical power like charisma. I don't buy it.

Pete: OK.

Bryn: OK, well what about leaders? They must have some charisma in order for people to follow them.

Joan: Are you kidding? I'd say about nought point nought nought one percent of politicians are charismatic. Most of them have lots of money behind them and a big political party that tells them what to say and wear and do, and how many babies to kiss.

Bryn: I never knew you were so cynical, Joan.

Pete: Wow, that's a bit of an eye-opener. You're really not into the rich and famous, are you ...

6.3

3 Read the texts. Choose the best words to complete them.

Smart cop
All morning an instructor had been explaining leadership to a group of police recruits, (1) _____ they were tired and hungry. Finally, the instructor gave one man secret instructions that he had to 'get everyone out of here without causing panic'. The recruit didn't know what to do. The instructor called a second man to the front. (2) _____ the note, the recruit said, 'The instructor wants us to go outside. Go!' No one moved. A third man looked at the instructions, smiled and said, 'Break for lunch!' (3) _____ the room emptied in seconds.

Blair overcomes the blues
Tony Blair was already a leader at university. (4) _____ term, his band Ugly Rumours were booked to play a concert. It (5) _____ when the drum kit fell off stage. As the others looked on in horror, Blair, in purple trousers, grabbed the microphone. 'Are you having a good time?' he shouted. 'I can't hear you at the back!' (6) _____ the drum disaster, the crowd responded and the show went on.

Thirsty soldiers
(7) _____ marching across the desert with his thirsty army, Alexander the Great was offered a helmet of water by one of his soldiers. Alexander said, 'Is there enough for 10,000 men?' The soldier had no answer, and (8) _____ Alexander was dying of thirst himself, he poured the water onto the ground.

A new page
Incredibly (9) _____, Google is no traditional workplace and co-founder Larry Page is said to be a charismatic as well as unorthodox boss. Page once made the staff attend a meeting wearing pink wigs, and he even tried to ban phones from a Google building. (10) _____, he was told that the law required a phone in the lifts.

1. A by this time B at this time C by which time
2. A By reading B On reading C To read
3. A at which point B at this point C to the point that
4. A While B In the middle C During
5. A had hardly begun B was already begun C had sooner begun
6. A Although B In spite C Despite
7. A During B While C On
8. A in spite of B much as C even though
9. A successful as is B successful as it is C as it is successful
10. A However B He'd hardly started C Even though

Vocabulary | describing people

4 Complete the crossword and find the key word. Look on page 84 of the Students' Book to help you.

Someone who ...

1. has a magnetic character that makes people want to follow (*adj*)
2. is well-respected because (s)he is calm and serious (*adj*)
3. believes people should live according to high moral standards and principles (*adj*)
4. is easy to talk to and friendly (*adj*)
5. never stops working because (s)he has lots of energy (*adj*)
6. can be trusted completely (*adj*)
7. is unable to make a decision, often _____ s (*v*)
8. accepts money illegally for favours (*adj*)
9. is energetic and determined, has _____ (*n*)
10. is not recognisable or interesting (*adj*)
11. is practical and direct in a sensible, honest way (*adj*)
12. is respected for his/her intellectual seriousness, has _____ (*n*)
13. is determined and won't change his/her mind (*adj*)

    Key word _____

49

Review and consolidation unit 6

Articles

1 There are one or two mistakes in each sentence. Find the mistakes and correct them.

1. The dogs are generally considered the best pets for the elderly.
2. We thought we heard burglar, but later we realised that a noise was actually the pipes.
3. He climbed the Mount Kilimanjaro when he was still the teenager.
4. As a child, she learned to play a piano and later went on to become the composer.
5. I'll see you in a supermarket at 8.00. Don't be late!
6. It's hard for the people like me to diet, because I love the chocolate.
7. UK has introduced law to help newly-arrived immigrants to find work.
8. I dreamed that I crossed Pacific Ocean in an old wooden boat!
9. Italian national anthem is one of my favourites.
10. We spoke to Chief Executive of the company last night.

whatever/whoever/whenever

2 Tick (✓) the correct sentence(s) in each pair. Both may be correct.

1. A Who you are, come out now with your hands up! ☐
   B Whoever you are, come out now with your hands up! ☐
2. A However hard I tried, it was never good enough for my father. ☐
   B How hard I tried, it was never good enough for my father. ☐
3. A You'll need to explain whatever you did, in very clear English. ☐
   B You'll need to explain what you did, in very clear English. ☐
4. A When you want to pop round, just give me a call. ☐
   B Whenever you want to pop round, just give me a call. ☐
5. A It seems that whichever option we take, it's going to be costly. ☐
   B It seems that which option we take, it's going to be costly. ☐
6. A This penknife will be useful where you're going. ☐
   B This penknife will be useful wherever you're going. ☐

Link words of time and contrast

3 Circle the correct word or expression.

A friend forever

Desperate thief Nick Bines broke into the home of a wealthy businessman, intending to steal jewellery and other valuables. He had (1) *hardly/sooner* begun the burglary when he looked at the sideboard and, to his surprise, saw himself in a framed photo. The photo showed a group of teenagers on a fishing trip. Bines went to the living room and looked at other photos on display, (2) *although/at which point* he realised that he was robbing the home of his best friend from school, Roger Farmer, whom he hadn't seen for ten years. (3) *Much/Hard* as he needed the money, Bines decided to put everything back in its place. He had begun to climb out of the window (4) *whilst/when* he caught his leg on the frame, fell and broke his ankle. He (5) *had no sooner/by this time* started crawling away along the side of the street than Roger Farmer's car pulled up. (6) *Although/On* seeing his old friend in this state, Farmer took Bines inside. (7) *In spite of the fact/While* they were talking, it soon became obvious what had happened. (8) *In spite/Despite* of this, instead of reporting his old friend to the police, Farmer took Bines to hospital and a month later gave him a job.

4 Match the sentence halves.

1. I'd walked for six hours, at ☐
2. Much as I love him, ☐
3. I passed the exam in spite ☐
4. I'd no sooner ☐
5. Although my alarm didn't go off, ☐
6. I'd hardly started my journey ☐
7. It took me until 2.00 to find her number, by which ☐
8. Desperately though I ☐

a. when my tyre exploded.
b. tried, I just couldn't finish the race.
c. taken off my coat than it started raining.
d. time she'd arrived.
e. of the fact that I'd been feeling awful before.
f. I still woke up early.
g. which point I was absolutely starving.
h. I really don't want to get married now.

50

Phrasal verbs

5 Rewrite the sentences using the correct form of the word in brackets.

1. You must stay up-to-date with developments in your field. (keep)
   You must _____ .
2. Those trousers are trendy at the moment. (in)
   Those trousers _____ .
3. The idea originated because of something I read. (come)
   The idea _____ .
4. The company is targeting the children's market. (home)
   The company is _____ .
5. It's hard to keep generating new ideas all the time. (with)
   It's hard to keep _____ .
6. That fashion will grow popular very quickly. (catch)
   That fashion will _____ .
7. His appearance on MTV in those shoes started a major new trend. (kick)
   His appearance on MTV in those shoes _____ .
8. Style gurus tell us that long hair is no longer fashionable. (out)
   Style gurus tell us that long hair _____ .

Vocabulary

6 Read the text. Choose the best words to complete it.

Chad Thomson is (1) _____ speaker – he had the audience in the palm of his hand at the Clovell Centre on Tuesday. His theme was that business leaders no longer have to be incredibly (2) _____ : the era of the Superhero CEO is over. Leaders today need to be (3) _____ and (4) _____ in order to understand the challenges faced by workers. Bosses that remain (5) _____ , locking themselves away in the office, are less effective. Thomson also said that (6) _____ leaders who regularly work 18-hour days are disappearing. His other theme was decision-making. Leaders who (7) _____ in the face of problems are not real leaders, while those who remain (8) _____ while under pressure are.

1. A a gravitas   B an inspiring   C an aloof
2. A nondescript   B dignity   C charismatic
3. A corrupt   B approached   C approachable
4. A down-to-earth B charisma   C lacking in energy
5. A inspirational B idealistic   C aloof
6. A trustworthy   B tireless   C tiring
7. A wave   B drive   C waver
8. A powerful   B resolute   C trusted

7 Complete the news headlines using words from the box.

> consumer   brain   in positions   solar
> comes to   world   special powers

1. Scientists hail _____ power as answer to energy crisis.
2. Ten-year-old genius uses _____ power to solve ancient puzzle!
3. China fast emerging as the new _____ power.
4. Supermarket boss says _____ power is forcing food companies to 'go organic' as customers walk away.
5. Report says corruption is on the rise among people _____ of power.
6. Democratic Party _____ power after twenty years in the wilderness.
7. Government grants _____ to anti-terrorist squad.

8 Add the correct words to the sentences.

1. We are setting these rules because we have at heart.
   A your interests   B your interest   C the interests
2. Sorry, but you need to. You just aren't good enough.
   A hear the music   B see the music   C face the music
3. Cheryl's found a great new job. She always seems to.
   A jump on her feet   B land with her feet   C land on her feet
4. I'm at these things so I'll show you what to do.
   A an old foot   B an old hand   C an old heart
5. On Friday the problem finally.
   A came to the head   B came with a head   C came to a head
6. Can you help me with this photocopying? I'm absolutely off my feet.
   A pushed   B rushed   C exhausted
7. We solved the problem and managed to
   A save the music   B save face   C keep face
8. When I saw my disastrous exam result, my.
   A head sank   B heart swam   C heart sank
9. That company went bankrupt because the boss didn't have a good.
   A head for business   B brain for business   C head in business
10. Sorry, she can't help you. She has.
    A her hand full   B her arms full   C her hands full

51

7.1 Nature

Reading

1 a Read the text and tick (✓) the correct answers.

1 What do Jiggs, Bart, Rock of Gibraltar and Keela have in common?
 A They are animals that have all appeared in films. ☐
 B They are animals that make a lot of money. ☐
 C They are animals with exceptional skills. ☐

2 Why might the chief constable of the South Yorkshire Police Force be jealous of Keela?
 A Because she is regarded as 'the star' of the South Yorkshire Police Force. ☐
 B Because other police forces want to use her skills and not his. ☐
 C Because Keela makes more money than him. ☐

3 What do the police use Keela for?
 A To help find victims of crime. ☐
 B To help train other dogs. ☐
 C To solve crimes involving blood. ☐

4 What were the FBI interested in?
 A Hiring Keela. ☐
 B Using Keela's training regime to train other dogs. ☐
 C Working with the South Yorkshire Police Force. ☐

b Find words in the text that mean:
1 paid for a job/service (v) (para 1) _____
2 very small amounts of something (n) (para 2) _____
3 cleaned (by rubbing it) (v) (para 2) _____
4 extremely small (adj) (para 2) _____
5 to improve a skill so that it is done very well (v) (para 3) _____
6 no angry thoughts even though you have … (three words, idiomatic) (para 4) _____

c Cover the text. Match a word from A to a word from B to make phrases from the text.

A: chief training crime sense dog film washing in

B: star constable of smell powder scene handlers regime demand

d Complete the summary of the text. Use the phrases you made in Ex. 1c.

She may not be a (1) _____ like other high-earning animals, but Keela is similarly (2) _____ . She has an incredible (3) _____ ; she can detect blood even after clothes have been washed in (4) _____ . This makes her especially useful at a (5) _____ . Once the (6) _____ realised she was so exceptional, they invented a special (7) _____ for her. She now makes more money than the (8) _____ of the police force!

The dog with the golden nose

(1) Jiggs, the chimpanzee that starred in over fifteen Tarzan films in the 1930s, was paid thousands of pounds. The owner of Bart, an Alaskan brown bear, was paid a million dollars for letting Bart appear in the film *The Edge*. A racehorse called Rock of Gibraltar is worth an estimated £100 million. And now there is Keela, a dog doing a great job and getting well remunerated for it.

(2) The spaniel is no film star, but she has become so important for South Yorkshire Police that she now earns more than the chief constable. The secret of her success? Keela has an astonishing sense of smell. She can sniff traces of blood on weapons that have been scrubbed clean after attacks and even on clothes that have been washed repeatedly in biological washing powder. PC Ellis, Keela's handler, said, 'She can detect minute quantities of blood that cannot be seen with the human eye. She is used at crime scenes where someone has tried to clean it up.'

(3) Once they realised Keela had these extraordinary skills, the dog handlers used a special training regime to hone her talent. In fact, her training was so successful that the FBI has inquired about it.

(4) Not surprisingly, Keela is in demand with other crime-busters. For her services, other police forces are charged £530 a day, plus expenses. She earns the South Yorkshire Police Force around £200,000 a year, more than PC Hughes, her boss! Hughes says there are no hard feelings. 'Keela's training gives the police force an edge when it comes to forensic investigation which we should recognise and use more often.'

52

Grammar | relative clauses

2 Choose the correct words to complete the sentences.

1 John and Kit, _____ missed the test yesterday, are here today.
   A both of whom   B both of whose
   C of both who

2 Jan wants to eat in Bob's Kitchen or King Curry House, _____ appeals to me.
   A neither which   B of neither which
   C neither of which

3 I met the writer Kate Atkinson, _____ books made such an impression on me.
   A of which   B whose   C with whose

4 The lead actor, _____ the show depended, didn't turn up.
   A who on   B on whom   C who

5 The police found the weapon _____ Mr Bloodgrind had killed his victim.
   A with which   B which   C which had

6 Carrie left early, _____ seems strange to me as she usually loves parties.
   A that   B which   C who

7 Zadie, _____ five children are brilliant mathematicians, is hopeless at maths.
   A of whose   B who's   C all of whose

8 The party leader _____ was asked to justify himself, could not.
   A when   B who   C while

3 Complete the sentences using ideas from the box, plus *who/when/which*, etc. You may need to add a preposition.

There were a hundred guests, most ...

There were a hundred guests, most of whom I'd already met.

> brother/work/with my wife   know/the way
> I/pay for   eat/all/chocolate   be/interested
> work OK/now

1 It was Juan _____ .
   That's why he's feeling sick!

2 When I was lost, I asked four people, none
   _____ .

3 These are the books _____
   _____ . These two were free.

4 Last week, we fixed these computers, all
   _____ .

5 This form must be completed before the conference. Please tick the topic in _____
   _____ .

6 I spoke to the woman _____ .

Vocabulary | collocations

4 One word in each sentence belongs in another sentence. Find the words and put them in the correct sentences.

1 By watching the movements of animals, we can predict natural safety such as earthquakes and tidal waves.

2 There are many stories of drowning people being carried to instincts by dolphins; these may be true because dolphins rescue animals the same size as themselves.

3 Animal disasters often allow animals to escape from danger that humans don't notice.

4 Rescue teams work with dogs because of the dogs' excellent invisible of smell.

5 Birds used to save sense during wartime by carrying vital messages to army commanders.

6 In the dark, cats and bats see things that are lives to the human eye.

How to ... | explain procedures

5 Complete the text. Add words from the box.

> this   straightforward   tricky   step   if
> once   put   got   of   at

Teaching a parrot to talk

Olaf Sund says that teaching a parrot to talk is a piece cake. Here he gives a few invaluable tips.

The first thing you've to do is choose the right bird. Bigger birds, like Blue Fronts and Yellow Napes, are your best bet, and make sure you get them when they are young. Birds older than eighteen months probably won't learn to talk.

You've chosen the bird, put it in the room where the family congregates the most – maybe the living room. For parrots to learn how to talk, human interaction is the key.

First it can be a bit for any wild animal in a domestic environment, so give the bird a few weeks to acclimatise. The next is to turn off the TV and remove any distractions. Place the bird on your hand and say a word in conjunction with an action or object. For example, give it a peanut and say: 'Peanut' or lift the bird up and say: 'Up'. The process must be pretty, so use short, simple words at first.

Be gentle and patient with the bird and lots of emotion in your voice. Teach the bird in fifteen-minute sessions, and give rewards such as food when the bird repeats a word. Without doing, some birds are slow to speak. Your teaching doesn't work, you should allow another family member to try. Many birds prefer a female voice.

7.2

Reading and Listening

1 **a** 🔊 7.1 Read and listen to three extracts from *Nature's extremes: places beyond man's dreams* by Walter McBryde. Write questions for the answers.

1 _____ ?
   In Sudan.
2 _____ ?
   Because they know where the water is.
3 _____ ?
   Because, by looking at them, you will see how the landscape has changed over millions of years.
4 _____ ?
   Like a person or animal roaring.
5 _____ ?
   Behind the water, next to the rock face.
6 _____ ?
   Captain Cook's.
7 _____ ?
   60,000 years old.
8 _____ ?
   Because a coral reef is actually alive.

b Answer the questions.

Death Valley
1 Why does Mr Bryde mention a man frying an egg on a car?
2 Why do you think he says 'You grow a new skin'?

The Iguaçu Falls
3 What images connected with the voice does Mr Bryde use to describe the Iguaçu Falls?
4 Why does he 'wonder if [the birds] can ever hear themselves sing'?

The Great Barrier Reef
5 Mr Bryde calls the Great Barrier Reef 'a million jewels'. What do you think he means?

c Find words in the text that mean:
1 area of land (4047 square metres) (extract 1) _____
2 burning brightly (extract 1) _____
3 crawl desperately, with your face to the ground (extract 1) _____
4 an enormous hole in the surface of the earth (extract 2) _____
5 forced into a small space (extract 2) _____
6 waterfall (extract 2) _____
7 water flying in small drops (extract 2) _____
8 crashed (extract 3) _____
9 long pieces of heavy wood used in buildings and ships (extract 3) _____
10 clear, transparent, allowing light to pass through (extract 3) _____

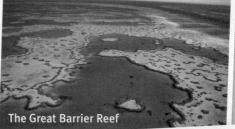
The Great Barrier Reef

The Iguaçu Falls

Death Valley

1: Death Valley
Don't get me wrong. I've seen a man fry an egg on the bonnet of his car in Arizona. I've seen birds drop dead out of the sky from the heat. I've seen acres of cracked Sudanese earth and the jawbone of a wildebeest fifty miles from the nearest water. But nothing can prepare you for Death Valley in the depths of a blazing summer. Everywhere you look, the air is shaking like fire. You grovel for water, following the trails of wise animals, keeping your distance. You grow a new skin, like leather.

The joy of Death Valley is in the rocks. Look closely and you'll see the history of the world. Burned into those rocks are the stories of climate change, the mutations of wind, water and gravity since the beginning of time.

2: The Iguaçu Falls
What hits you first is the sound. Long before you get close, you hear the roaring, like some great giant's endless breath. As you approach, it gets louder, until finally you see it – a vast chasm beyond your imagining, endless tongues of screaming white water and spray rebounding a hundred feet into the air. The Iguaçu Falls. I look over the edge and I see behind the water, jammed against the rock, birds' nests! A whole colony of them. They made their home in the middle of the world's biggest cataract. And now, twisting like corkscrews from under the spray, the birds rise free into the air and float above us. I wonder if they can ever hear themselves sing.

3: The Great Barrier Reef
In 1770, Captain Cook's boat rammed smack into the reef. A barrel of rum fell overboard and sank. Little did he know that underneath the wooden beams of his ship there was a world of such magnificence, such translucent light and life. The Great Barrier Reef is a million jewels. Flatback turtles and humpback whales, dolphins and clownfish and giant clams with sprawling shells. The Great Barrier Reef is a poem to itself: 2000 kilometres long and 60,000 years old, 900 islands and 3000 coral reefs. They say you can see it from space.

I duck beneath the water for the twentieth time, the aqualung heavy on my back. I am still trying to believe my eyes. The water is like a glass kaleidoscope, a riot of colour. This is the biggest living organism in the world and I am swimming in its blue heart.

Grammar | verb patterns

2 Match the sentences.

1. 1 She remembers talking to Joe. ☐
   2 She remembered to talk to Joe. ☐
   A At the last party she accidentally ignored him.
   B They were outside the library.

2. 1 I regret telling you about the accident. ☐
   2 I regret to tell you about the accident. ☐
   A I should have kept it a secret.
   B Fortunately, nobody has been seriously hurt.

3. 1 Willy tried drinking the special remedy, ☐
   2 Willy tried to drink the special remedy, ☐
   A but he couldn't swallow it because it was so disgusting.
   B but it didn't cure him of his illness.

4. 1 A week on that boat means making ☐
   2 A week on that boat is meant to make ☐
   A you feel wonderful.
   B your own entertainment because there's nothing to do there.

5. 1 The old man stopped listening to the birds. ☐
   2 The old man stopped to listen to the birds. ☐
   A They were singing beautifully so he stayed there for a while.
   B They were making such a terrible noise that he couldn't stand it any more.

6. 1 As the children liked his first game, ☐
   2 After buying his first Lego set at the age of eight, ☐
   A he went on inventing games all afternoon until everyone had had enough.
   B he went on to invent lots of games, and eventually he became famous.

3 Complete the text using the correct form of words from the box.

> become go make experience
> take travel leave stay

Vocabulary | description

4 Match the sentence halves.

1. After an hour in the heat of Delhi, Elsie was drenched ☐
2. Fish River Canyon probably has the most spectacular ☐
3. I thought Siberia would have been too cold for permanent ☐
4. Disneyland is one of the world's most visited tourist ☐
5. There are a number of active ☐
6. Death Valley in California is 282 feet below ☐
7. Many places in Arkansas became ghost ☐
8. I like Rio's vibrant ☐
9. We were absolutely parched, ☐
10. If you trespass on ☐

a volcanoes in Italy, including Mount Vesuvius.
b in sweat and desperate for water.
c someone else's land, you can be arrested.
d so we bought several bottles of water.
e towns after a terrible epidemic killed 70,000 people.
f landscape in Africa. It's the world's second biggest canyon.
g nightlife. There's always a party going on somewhere.
h settlement, but there are large communities that live there.
i sites – millions see it every year.
j sea level.

Life choices

She remembered (1) _____ that photo. It was the first day of her trip in the desert. While her friends were content to sit on a beach during their holidays, she always tried (2) _____ new customs, new places, new people. She used to say, 'The day I stop (3) _____ the world is the day I die.' Her parents thought she would go on (4) _____ either a travel writer or a tour guide, but instead one day she just never returned. On a trip to Egypt she had stopped (5) _____ for a camel ride near the Pyramids in Cairo. She had never meant (6) _____ longer than a day or two, but as she watched the sun slowly falling over the sand dunes, casting them in a sea of orange, she fell in love with the desert and vowed to stay. It meant (7) _____ behind the safe world that she had known all her life, but now, forty years later, sitting at her home in Alexandria, looking over the photos, it was a choice she had never regretted (8) _____ .

7.3

Grammar | *as ... as* and describing quantity

1 Match the questions to the answers.
1 How many pictures should we take? ☐
2 Who's going to be there? ☐
3 What do the expensive tickets cost? ☐
4 How far is it to Jacksonville? ☐
5 Do you go there regularly? ☐
6 What have you heard about me? ☐
7 How tall is he? ☐
8 Can I have some of your water? ☐

a Yes, as much as you like.
b Over $100.
c Virtually everyone.
d Virtually nothing.
e Well under ten kilometres.
f Approximately two metres.
g As many as we can.
h As often as possible.

2 Add the correct words and phrases to the sentences.
1 This one's cheaper than that one.
   A a great deal **B** a deal **C** a load
2 I'm told that all of them passed – only two people had to retake the exam.
   A majority **B** precisely **C** virtually
3 Our courses cost $224.99 per week, an absolute bargain!
   A as much as **B** as many as
   C as little as
4 Your suitcase weighs exactly fifty kilos, which is the limit!
   A well over **B** much above
   C a minimum
5 This lift takes ten people.
   A a majority of **B** a maximum of
   C virtually
6 A people wanted Jones to win, but everyone else voted for Smith.
   A small majority **B** tiny minority of
   C few of
7 During the winter, we sometimes get six or seven tourist groups a week.
   A as little as **B** a great deal of
   C as few as
8 I need one hundred and twenty-three of those bottles. No more, no less!
   A precisely **B** approximately
   C a minimum of

Pronunciation | *as* (weak form)

3 ▶ 7.2 Cover the tapescript. Listen and repeat. Use the weak form /ə/ for *as* where appropriate.

> **TAPESCRIPT**
> It's as good as new.
> It's as big as a house.
> It's as cold as ice.
> It's as clean as a whistle.
> It's as good as you'll find anywhere.
> It's as fast as a train.

Vocabulary | buying and selling

4 There are two mistakes in each monologue. Find and correct them.

1 'Well, yes, it's used, but it's in great condition. This really is a rare opportunity because it's a latest model, as I'm sure you realise. Everything's in working order, though I haven't tried the brakes yet. And don't worry about that tear and wear on the tyres. They'll be fine.'

2 'This one is a very rare opal stone. It really is one in a kind. Over a thousand years ago it was probably worn by a tribal queen. Despite its age, you can see that it is in perfect conditions.'

3 'These are all made to hand. We pick the fruit in the morning, chop it up and coat it in sugar and honey. Then we roll the pastry and put the fruit inside it. You can choose from a selecting of over fifteen fruits.'

4 'This model has only been on the markets for a few weeks and it's unbelievable: you've got wide-screen vision, anti-reflection technology, and it even features an intelligent remote control that knows your viewing tastes. It's absolutely state-in-the-art and it's yours, brand new, for just $10,000.'

5 'OK, OK, they're second-hand but they're as well as new. I mean, look, they're still in their packaging! They come in a wide arrangement of colours and sizes, and the lenses are just fantastic. What do you mean, "the sun's not going to come out"?'

56

Writing

5 Choose one of the pictures below. Imagine you are selling the item(s) on eBay. Write the advertisement.

Listening

6 a Read the statements. Tick (✓) the response that best describes your view.

1 Scientists should be banned from doing medical experiments on animals.

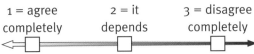

1 = agree completely   2 = it depends   3 = disagree completely

2 People who mistreat their pets should go to prison.

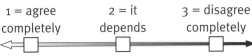

1 = agree completely   2 = it depends   3 = disagree completely

3 Animals should not be put in circuses or used for other forms of entertainment.

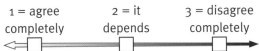

1 = agree completely   2 = it depends   3 = disagree completely

b 7.3 Cover the tapescript. Listen to three people who work with animals and answer the questions.

1 What is his/her job?
2 Has the speaker (or his/her profession) been criticised? If so, what for?
3 Does the speaker justify this treatment of animals? If so, how?
4 How does the interviewer feel about the issue? How do we know?

TAPESCRIPT

1

I: Jennifer, you say your profession is under attack, but isn't it the mice, the monkeys, the animals, that are suffering?

J: I realise the ethics of it aren't simple, but to have people burning down laboratories, threatening the families of scientists is really something else altogether.

I: Three million experiments on animals were conducted in Britain alone last year, in the name of science. How can we possibly justify those sort of numbers?

J: Well, firstly I would dispute those figures. But the main point is that the experiments are for the benefit of humankind. Without them, modern medicine would be in medieval times and we'd all be dying of common colds. No one wants to harm an animal intentionally, but you have to weigh up a number of issues. There are a lot of …

2

I: Heather, you've written, and I'm quoting here, that you 'see the darker side of humanity every day'. Can you explain what you mean by that?

H: Well, what I mean is that in my job, working for the RSPCA, a charity that protects animals, I go wherever I'm called, wherever there are abuses of animals, and some of the things I see are really quite shocking.

I: Could you give us an example?

H: I could give you thousands. A week ago, I visited a home because a neighbour had heard a whining sound and scratching against a wall. I discovered that a family had locked up a large dog in a four-by-four-foot cupboard for one week, without giving it food or water, and for no discernible reason. So that's what I mean by the darker side of humanity.

I: It seems impossible in this day and age that these things can still happen. So can you tell us a bit more about …

3

J: It had always been one of the great traditions of our circus, but eventually the pressure became too great.

I: And that's why you stopped using animals?

J: For myself, and a number of other circus managers, it was obvious that times had changed. But it wasn't an easy decision to get rid of animals from our act.

I: What effects has the decision had?

J: Well, the first thing was that I had to fire about fifty members of staff whose job was looking after or training the animals, and that was very tough for them and me. The second thing was that little children would come along to the circus expecting to see monkeys and elephants and sea lions, and they wouldn't be there.

I: Do you believe it was wrong to use the animals in the circus, when we know they were taken from their natural environment and basically captured and trained to entertain people?

J: No. The animals were treated extremely well. It was pressure from outside that forced the decision on me.

Review and consolidation unit 7

Vocabulary

1 Find words in Unit 7 of the Students' Book that match the definitions.

a_____ = many medical scientists do _____ testing before testing medicines on humans (n)
b_____ = animals do this to have offspring (v) OR particular type in a species of animal (n)
c_____ = meat eater (n)
d_____ = animal that guards (n)
e_____ = _____ species are types of animal which may become extinct soon (adj)
f_____ = the _____ trade uses precious animal skin for clothing (n)
g_____ = _____ dogs help the blind (n)
h_____ = what many animals do during winter months (v)
i_____ = animal _____ allow animals to sense danger (n)
k_____ = an Australian animal with grey fur (n)
l_____ = birds _____ eggs (v)
m_____ = animal that feeds its young with milk from its body, e.g. cows, humans (n)
n_____ = an animal's _____ habitat is the place where wild animals live (n)
o_____ = when humans catch too many fish in one place, leading to changes in the ecosystem (v)
p_____ = any animal that hunts another (n)
r_____ = a nature _____ is an area of land where wild animals are protected (n)
s_____ = area for birds or animals where they are safe and can't be hunted (n)
t_____ = not wild
v_____ = you and your pet may need one to avoid diseases (n)
w_____ = spider's home and where you can buy animals illegally! (n)

Relative clauses

2 Choose the correct words and phrases to finish the sentences. Both alternatives may be correct.

1 I went to greet the children, some
   A of whom I'd already met.
   B of them I'd already met.
2 We visited the two proposed sites,
   A of which neither was suitable.
   B neither of which was suitable.
3 I went bowling last night,
   A that was enjoyable.   B which was enjoyable.
4 That's the multinational conglomerate
   A for which she worked.   B which she worked for.
5 That's the singer
   A whose CD you're always playing.
   B who's CD you're always playing.
6 There must be a hundred lights in here,
   A none of them work.   B none of which work.
7 We are walking the same path
   A that Robert Frost walked.   B which Robert Frost walked.
8 This is one law
   A which we all benefit from.   B from which we all benefit.
9 It's a profession
   A in that I hope to succeed.   B in which I hope to succeed.
10 The stadium was full of people,
   A most of whom supported Brazil.
   B most of which supported Brazil.

Verb patterns

3 Complete the sentences by adding the infinitive or gerund form of words from the box.

| warn play spill inform become smoke pay |
| drink feed leave buy talk |

1 I decided to stop because my lungs were in bad shape.
2 That sweet little boy went on President.
3 They regretted so much money for such a terrible meal.
4 Will you remember the cat while I'm away?
5 I tried you about that horrible man but you wouldn't listen.
6 During the trip we stopped petrol a couple of times.
7 We asked her to be quiet but she just went on throughout the film.
8 It was an accident – I didn't mean that water all over her computer!
9 Do you remember that game when we were children?
10 She tried hot milk before bed, but nothing would work – she still couldn't sleep.
11 This new job means our hometown to go and live abroad.
12 I regret you that your contract has been terminated with immediate effect.

58

Vocabulary

4 Read the text. Choose the best words to complete it.

Earthquake!

Ten minutes after the earthquake struck, the (1) _____ ran into the remains of the building, which was located close to a (2) _____ . They were there to (3) _____ . Again and again they removed huge chunks of brick, and carried the injured (4) _____ . They didn't normally deal with (5) _____ like earthquakes. The dangers they (6) _____ were usually due to human error – people getting trapped in lifts, stupid things like that – but it didn't (7) _____ to them. Lives were lives. When it seemed as if there was no more to be done, one of the men sensed a movement, something almost (8) _____ the human eye. They had combed every inch of the building, but the man's (9) _____ going in there. Within minutes he emerged carrying a tiny cat. The cat's (10) _____ had told it to hide under a cupboard, where it had subsequently become trapped.

1. A rescuing team B rescue squad C rescue team
2. A tourist site B touristic area C tourism site
3. A safe lives B be saved lives C save lives
4. A safely B to safety C for safety
5. A nature disasters B nature's disasters C natural disasters
6. A faced B touched C made
7. A make the difference B mean any difference C make any difference
8. A invisible to B invisible for C invisible with
9. A heart was decided on B heart was set on C head was set on
10. A animal's instinct B intelligent instincts C animal instincts

as ... as and describing quantity

5 Complete the words.

1. We found that a large m_____ of people (nearly ninety percent) wanted to change their job.
2. V_____ none (0.3 percent) of the people felt that they would be in the same job for the rest of their life.
3. A small m_____ (around three percent) said they had applied for a new job in the last month.
4. As f_____ as thirteen percent of participants claimed that they would like to go (back) to university.
5. Most of the participants had been in work for ap_____ ten to fifteen years.
6. Thirty percent said their salary is w_____ u_____ what they deserve, and want more money.
7. 0.1 percent feel they are paid a g_____ d_____ of money for not doing much.
8. Sixty percent believe they will be in their current job for a mi_____ of two more years.

Vocabulary

6 a Match the sentence halves.

1. It's in ☐
2. It's as ☐
3. It's the ☐
4. It's state- ☐
5. It's on ☐
6. It's made ☐
7. It's one ☐
8. It has some ☐
9. It comes in a ☐
10. It's brand ☐

a wide range of colours.
b by hand.
c of-the-art.
d new.
e of a kind.
f the market.
g wear and tear.
h good as new.
i latest model.
j excellent condition.

b Write the expressions from Ex. 6a that have similar meanings to:

1. You can choose from a selection. _____
2. It's handcrafted. _____
3. It's still in its packaging. _____
4. It's unique. _____
5. It's available now. _____

7 a Put the words in the correct order to make sentences.

1. breaking up tricky a fight can dog very be
   ☐ _____ .
2. if hit will it you you dog attack the,
   ☐ _____ .
3. the next to do walk dog is to thing you've the backwards got
   ☐ _____ .
4. finally from the away dogs other each tie,
   ☐ _____ .
5. secondly help get,
   ☐ _____ .
6. firstly hit dog the don't,
   ☐ _____ .
7. once you've dog's the help grab hind legs got,
   ☐ _____ .

b Number the sentences above 1–7 in the correct order.

59

8.1 Issues

Listening

1 a 8.1 Cover the tapescript. Listen to a radio programme called *Future world* and choose the best summary.

Future world describes ...

1 problems we will have in the future, and possible technological solutions.
2 some new inventions that may help people in the future.
3 ways in which technology has improved the lives of ordinary people.

b Listen again. Mark the statements true (T) or false (F).

1 V2V involves cars 'talking to each other' through a computer system. ☐
2 The new mobile phone will tell you how nervous or confident you look. ☐
3 The new mobile phone was invented to help people during 'speed dates'. ☐
4 The memory device is not just one machine. ☐
5 According to Gordon Bell, recording your life is rather dull, but may be important in the future. ☐

c Put the words from the box into the right columns. Look at the tapescript to help you.

> unintelligible   gadget
> pedal   gizmo   steering wheel
> husky   backseat driver
> hand-held device   censor
> squeaky   baritone   swerve

driving	
technology	
the voice	

TAPESCRIPT

A: What have you got for us, Joe?
J: Well, we have a stunning selection of gadgets and gizmos for the future, including a car that can't crash, a mobile phone that tells you you're never going to get a date if you talk like that! And some software that will allow you to carry years and years of memories in your pocket. How about that?
A: Sounds terrifying.
J: It isn't.
A: So tell us about the car. What is it and how does it work?
J: We're entering James Bond territory here. The system is called V2V.
A: V2V. Sounds like a disease.
J: V2V stands for 'vehicle to vehicle communication'. Basically, we're talking about sensors on the side of the road that will exchange information with your car about what other cars are doing. Not only that, but the car will also swerve for you to avoid a crash. We're talking about a backseat driver, but one that's always right!
A: Brilliant. Sounds like a lifesaver.
J: It is. They're even working on steering wheels that can shake sleepy drivers awake, and pedals that vibrate.
A: Fantastic. What about the mobile phone?
J: Well, this is a different kind of lifesaver. It's going to be a big help to shy young men trying to get a date.
A: How's that then?
J: It's a socially aware mobile phone that can analyse voice patterns and tell you if you sound nervous or cool. It can tell you if you're speaking too fast or if you're unintelligible, or even if your voice is too squeaky! It was recently piloted at a speed dating session and guess what?
A: What?
J: The participants loved it!
A: Very interesting, though I always thought it was good looks that got you a first date.
J: Never underestimate the importance of having a husky baritone!
A: What about the memory stick?
J: It's not a memory stick! Those existed years ago.
A: Sorry, the memory device!
J: The memory device.
A: Tell us more.
J: It's actually a few devices: a mini-camera that can fit into a contact lens and a microphone that fits in your ear. You download the data onto a hand-held device and there you have it: a lifetime's worth of memories.
A: But who would want it?
J: Gordon Bell.
A: Who's he?
J: A researcher who's been recording his entire life since 1998 for a project called MyLifeBits.
A: Wow.
J: He scans all of his photos and documents, and records meetings, phone calls and emails, and he wears a mini-camera round his neck to get an image of everything he sees.
A: But isn't it unbelievably dull?
J: Well, according to Bell, it's similar to having an assistant with a perfect memory. But I imagine it depends on just how dull your life is!

8.1

Vocabulary | giving opinions

2 Complete the texts using words from the box.

> overrated indispensable do harm underrated
> waste lifesaver disastrous force benefits

I think guns do more (1) _____ than good. People all over the world are murdered using them. Overall, they've been (2) _____ for society: absolutely terrible!

I know that guns are dangerous in the wrong hands, but they are also a (3) _____ for good when used sensibly. Guns are completely (4) _____ if we want to protect ourselves, and they are literally a (5) _____ against criminals.

In my view, mobile phones are (6) _____. They are not a complete (7) _____ of space, but we don't really need them. In the past, we just made arrangements more carefully or used pay phones.

We can't (8) _____ without mobile phones. They have huge (9) _____ for society because they allow us to communicate more, which is a great thing. I actually think they are (10) _____; we don't realise how useful mobile phones are until we find ourselves in an emergency.

Grammar | reporting verbs

3 Choose the correct words or phrases to complete the sentences. Two alternatives may be possible.

1 She _____ to university, but he just wanted to find a job.
   A insisted Brian going   B encouraged Brian to go
   C suggested that Brian go
2 Davies _____ the money.
   A warned us to steal   B denied stealing
   C threatened to steal
3 Claudia _____ eating the cake, even though I was innocent.
   A accused me of   B threatened to   C blamed me for
4 I _____ I had been stupid.
   A admitted that   B confessed that   C informed that
5 Georgina _____ take our warm clothes.
   A encouraged that we   B told us to
   C reminded us to
6 He always _____ his record was the best.
   A accused that   B maintained that   C insisted on

4 Rewrite the sentences using the verbs in brackets.

1 Mr Blythe told us again to read the safety precautions. (remind)
   Mr Blythe _____.
2 'My advice is to call a doctor,' said Lena. (suggest)
   Lena _____.
3 We had taken it for granted that you knew each other. (assume)
   We _____.
4 She said Tom had stolen the apple. (accuse)
   She _____.
5 We had to say that we didn't know the answer. (admit)
   We _____.
6 I said 'well done' to her for passing her exam. (congratulate)
   I _____.
7 Dad said he'd stop our pocket money if we continue to behave badly. (threaten)
   Dad _____.
8 'I've never met her before!' said Clarence. (deny)
   Clarence _____.

How to ... | stall for time

5 Put the letters in *italics* in the correct order to make words. Then put B's words in the correct order to make sentences.

1 A: So what will you do next?
   B: a *nusqoiet* that's good _____.
2 A: Which of your male co-stars was your favourite?
   B: I of all them loved *lelw* _____.
3 A: Of all your films, which would you like to be remembered for?
   B: see *tel* me _____.
4 A: Do you regret starring in any of your films?
   B: I'd that about to *ikhnt* have _____.
5 A: Will you get married again for a sixth time?
   B: *rkctyi* that's _____.
6 A: Who was your favourite director?
   B: question that's *iitfcldfu* a _____.

8.2

Grammar | continuous and simple

1 Match the questions to the answers.

1 Why did she look so sad? ☐
2 Why did they look tired? ☐
3 Why are they such a mess? ☐
4 Why did the police stop him? ☐
5 What were all those people doing there? ☐
6 When did Johnny start his trip? ☐
7 Why isn't Anna Rita doing the course? ☐
8 What were all those secret meetings about? ☐
9 Why didn't Emma answer the phone? ☐
10 What's she doing in that room? ☐

a They were being taken on a short tour of the harbour.
b They'd been talking all night.
c They'd been thinking of selling the company.
d I think she's been playing computer games all evening.
e She may have been sleeping when you rang.
f He'll have been travelling for exactly two weeks this time tomorrow.
g He must have been driving too fast.
h She was going to a funeral.
i She's expecting a baby in one month!
j They've been painting the window frames.

2 Complete the text using the continuous or simple form of the verbs in brackets. If both are possible, use the continuous.

Words to the wise

My grandmother lived until she was 100. By the time she died, she (1) _____ (never/be) more than fifty kilometres from where she was born. A large, modest woman, she took enormous pride in her family and home. Out of that life came a lot of wisdom.

When I was in my twenties I worked in product research. I (2) _____ (have) problems at work for several months with a particular colleague and I wasn't sure what to do. One afternoon, while I (3) _____ (struggle) in the office, I decided to escape by visiting my grandmother for coffee and cake. She (4) _____ (sense) that something was on my mind. 'Theo, always do the worst things first,' she said.

'Thanks, Grandma,' I said. 'Can we have cake now?' On (5) _____ (return) to the office the following day, I confronted the colleague I (6) _____ (battle) with, and we resolved our differences. It was then that I realised my grandmother was right. If a situation (7) _____ (start) to get on top of you, delaying the solution will only make it worse. I started to schedule first the thing I (8) _____ (hate) doing the most. Once it is done, the rest of your day is wonderful. Normally, we (9) _____ (put off) the things we don't want to do until last, and it worries us all day and evening. I (10) _____ (follow) my grandmother's advice for over thirty years, and I've never regretted it.

Vocabulary | lifestyles

3 Complete the sentences using words from the box.

> security   out   hair   buzz   and   crashed

1 Because of stress and high expectations, many tennis players burn _____ before they reach thirty.
2 A lot of business people who are already rich and successful say that the main motivator is no longer money, but the _____ and excitement of doing deals.
3 After working for twenty hours non-stop, I _____ out on the sofa and didn't wake up until 11.30 the following morning.
4 Mark was tearing his _____ out with frustration when they overlooked him for promotion again.
5 Julie tries to save some money every week as a _____ blanket in case of unexpected disasters!
6 I don't think work should come before family; your career isn't the be-all _____ end-all.

Reading

4 a Read the ideas. Tick (✓) them once if you already do them. Tick (✓✓) twice if you would like to try them.

Twenty ways to beat stress

1. **Learn something new such as a sport, a language or a skill like painting. Short bursts of intense concentration are a great way to relieve stress.**
2. Teach yourself massage techniques, yoga or T'ai chi.
3. **Make the most of seasonal fruits such as strawberries, raspberries and cherries. They are full of feel-good nutrients.**
4. Pamper yourself once a week: watch a film, have a soothing bath with oils or buy yourself a bouquet of your favourite flowers.
5. **Write down something good that happened to you in each year of your life.**
6. Avoid sugary snacks and fizzy drinks that are likely to give you a temporary high. Drink water and snack on natural foods such as nuts instead.
7. **Call up your inner child, and do something you haven't done for years, like having a go on a swing or putting on an old pair of roller skates.**
8. Talk to someone about your problems. Bottling things up only makes them worse.
9. **If you have a sedentary job, do something physical like gardening or going for a run.**
10. Switch off every machine in the house, ignore all but the most urgent emails for twenty-four hours, get comfortable and read a book.
11. **Bake bread. Kneading dough is hard work but soothing, and the smell of fresh bread is guaranteed to lift your spirits.**
12. Get back to nature. Treat yourself to a long walk in a park.
13. **Meditate. Cultivate optimistic thoughts. Think of what you've got, not what you want.**
14. Get rid of all the clutter on your desk. Throw away everything you don't really need.
15. **Look through your wardrobe. If you haven't worn something for over eighteen months, give it to a charity or to someone who will wear it.**
16. Go to a Karaoke bar and sing away your worries. Alternatively, close all the doors, put on your favourite music at full volume and sing/dance until you're exhausted.
17. **Go to bed an hour earlier than usual to improve your sleep.**
18. Cut down on alcohol, nicotine and caffeine. Reduce your intake gradually and you may find that you can give it up altogether.
19. **Go home a different way. For instance, walk home from work if it's not too far.**
20. Eat at least one meal a day with friends or family.

b Find words from the text that mean:

1. sudden period of activity or noise (*n*) (para 1) _____
2. give someone lots of loving care and attention (e.g. buying them gifts, etc.) (*v*) (para 4) _____
3. makes you feel calm and less worried (*adj*) (para 4) _____
4. a feeling of having lots of energy or great happiness (*n*) (para 6) _____
5. not allow yourself to show feelings (*verb + preposition*) (para 8) _____
6. involving sitting down and not moving (*adj*) (para 9) _____
7. work hard to help something grow (*v*) (para 13) _____
8. things that fill space untidily and aren't necessary (*n*) (para 14) _____

c Complete the sentences using the correct form of the words you found in Ex. 4b.

1. I hated my _____ lifestyle, stuck behind a desk for eight hours a day, so I took up jogging.
2. Lyudmila went for a _____ massage every morning.
3. Don't _____ your problems. Tell me about them. You need to get them off your chest.
4. We need to remove useless _____ from our lives and to focus on what is essential.
5. My husband really _____ me. He buys me flowers and new clothes every week.
6. She's very good at _____ personal relationships. She writes letters, invites people to dinner and always keeps in touch.
7. Caffeine gives you a natural _____ , but you shouldn't have too much of it.
8. I completed all my work in a two-day _____ of energy!

8.3

Listening

1 a [8.2] Cover the tapescript. Listen to five phone messages. Take notes.

> **TAPESCRIPT**
>
> **1**
> Hi Joseph, it's Chris here. Just wanted to say that something's come up and, basically, I'm not going to be able to make it to your place by six, so I'll try and get there, erm, well, as soon as I can. It's a problem with the air conditioning here at the office and basically the only time the engineer can come is after five thirty, so I'm having to stay a bit late. Anyway, I'll be there as soon as possible. Bye.
>
> **2**
> Hello, it's Sandy here from Small World Travel. There's been a problem with your tickets to Fiji. Can you give me a call on 0207 933 6399. That's 0207 933 6399. Thank you.
>
> **3**
> Hello darling, it's me. If you get this message, can you try and get hold of Dominique about babysitting? I completely forgot to ask her yesterday and I don't have her phone number on me. Ummm, I suppose about seven till twelve as usual. Speak to you later.
>
> **4**
> Hello. I bought a Classic Body Toner Home Gym from you on Saturday, which was delivered on Monday, but there seems to be a problem with it. At the moment I can't get the machine to work at all, even though the guys who delivered it said it was easy and I've followed the instructions in the manual. Could you please send an engineer round as soon as possible because I really need to have it in working order immediately. By the way, my name is Alexandra Duvall and I've got the customer order number here. It's, um, 675637. Thank you.
>
> **5**
> James, it's Liz Jordan here. I've just had a message to say that our keynote speaker is ill and won't be able to come to the conference, so it's pretty urgent that we find a replacement. I haven't spoken to William yet, so if you could pass on this message. And give me a call. You can get hold of me on my mobile at any time. Bye.

b Listen again and answer the questions.

1 What exactly is the problem?
2 What exactly must the receiver of the message do?

Grammar | fronting

2 Choose the correct alternative.

Great_advice.com

My fiancée and I are planning our wedding. The (1) *matter/worrying/thing* is, we want a small, informal one (family and best friends only), but we don't want to offend people by not inviting them. The fact (2) *to the matter/remains/of the matter* is, they all invited us to their weddings and we feel a bit mean having a private one. **Alex**

Alex, I understand your concerns, but the (3) *matter/point/trouble* is, it's your special day and it's for you to decide how you want to spend it. Ignore all other considerations. Sajid

Hi Alex, One (4) *thing you could/option you could/way to* do is organise a party for all your friends a few weeks before you get married, and explain to them that you want a quiet wedding. Sue

Happy_to_help.com

My husband's son by his first marriage still lives at home although he is twenty-three. (5) *The thing irritates/The matter for/What irritates* me is that he doesn't work or study and he does nothing around the house, treating me like a servant. My husband keeps saying 'give him time' but my patience is running thin. (6) *What we need/What needs/The matter* to do is talk to him seriously about the situation, but my husband refuses. **Georgia**

Dear Georgia, Although your husband's attitude is, in some ways, understandable, the fact (7) *stays/remains that/remains* he needs to take the lead in this situation. He must talk to the boy. Kerry

Georgia, (8) *What could happen/What you could try/The trouble* is to set some rules about housework: draw up a rota that everyone has to follow. Joanne

Vocabulary | cause and effect

3 Read the text. Circle the best words to complete it.

As anyone who's ever waited in a long queue will testify, there's nothing like bad service to kill a business. It can also be a (1) *major source/big root/serious consequence* of stress when something goes wrong and no one seems willing to help. We've heard stories of people waiting on the phone for an hour before customer service answers, or people hanging on for weeks to get faulty equipment replaced. All of this has (2) *down-reaching/long-reaching/far-reaching* implications for businesses, because bad service (3) *develops/makes/breeds* dissatisfaction. The (4) *stem/result/cause* is that customers will go elsewhere next time, and also tell others their horror stories. Mark Bradley wrote a book called *Inconvenience Stores* about a year of customer service in the UK. The idea (5) *had it origins in/was originated in/was original in* some research Bradley was doing for a business presentation, but the fascinating anecdotes (6) *result in/had a result that/resulted in* increased interest and eventually he wrote a whole book. It doesn't make happy reading. At one point he asks for a café latte and is told 'You'll have to go to Leeds [another city] for that.' He concludes that much of the poor service (7) *has its roots/roots/gives rise* in the fact that employees have no power to make decisions. In one hotel chain, staff have to get permission to say no to customers. Naturally, this (8) *consequences/causes of/leads to* serious problems for the hotel. So how can businesses (9) *reach/bring about/breed* change in the form of better service? Bradley reckons companies need to improve morale among employees and give them the freedom to do what's right for the customer. The (10) *source/consequences/roots* could be wonderful for us all!

How to … | describe everyday problems

4 Complete the mini-dialogues by adding words from the box.

> appears   won't   switching   get   seem   showing

1 A: I'm having problems on the oven.
   B: Yes, there's something wrong with it.
2 A: I can't the washing machine to wash the clothes.
   B: That's because it's a drier!
3 A: The computer doesn't to be working.
   B: That's because you haven't switched it on.
4 A: The car still start.
   B: Let's call the mechanic.
5 A: The clock is always the wrong time.
   B: I know. It needs a new bat…
6 A: This light to be broken. It …
   B: I think the bulb's gone.

Writing

5 a Read the opening lines of an essay. Number the sentences 1–7 in the correct order to continue the essay.

> Procrastination affects most of us at some time or another. <u>For this reason</u>, a number of studies have been carried out looking into its causes and consequences. <u>Furthermore</u>, we have tried to develop and evaluate a number of possible solutions to the problem.

- [ ] The first cause we discovered was a lack of concentration.
- [ ] Consequently, putting it off just adds to that feeling of anxiety, because time is running out.
- [ ] For example, some perfectionists believe they must do extensive research before writing anything.
- [ ] Instead of dealing with the task at hand, many people let their mind wander, staring out of the window or surfing the net.
- [ ] This means that they read and read but never actually get round to writing the paper.
- [ ] A third cause is perfectionism.
- [ ] The second cause was fear; when we are worried that a task is beyond us, we tend to put it off.

b <u>Underline</u> useful linking and sequencing expressions. The first two have been done for you.

Review and consolidation unit 8

Reporting verbs

1 Read the story extract and complete the sentences. Use the words in brackets when they are given.

'Don't go in there,' said June. But they were determined to go. Mike, the oldest, said, 'Why should we listen to you anyway? You're just a kid!'

'It's haunted!' replied June. 'And if you go in there, I'll tell my mother!' Mike just laughed and said, 'You're lying.' But Sally was nervous.

'What if June's right?' she asked. Mike said, 'Don't be ridiculous. Ghosts don't exist. We'll be out of there in two minutes.'

'OK,' said Sally. As they approached the house, June ran the other way and shouted, 'Don't forget what happened to the dog!'

'Thanks!' said Mike, as he grabbed Sally's hand and stepped through the doorway. At that moment their lives changed, and nothing would ever be the same again.

1. June warned _____ . (the house)
2. June claimed _____ .
3. June threatened _____ .
4. Mike accused _____ .
5. Mike informed _____ . (ghosts)
6. Mike persuaded _____ . (go in)
7. Sally agreed _____ . (the house)
8. June reminded _____ .
9. Mike thanked _____ . (the warning)
10. Later they regretted _____ . (the house)

Vocabulary

2 Choose the correct words and phrases to finish the sentences.

1. I hate taking medicine. I think it does me
   A more harm than good.   B harm more than good.
   C more good than harm.
2. The book is nowhere near as interesting as I thought it would be. It's a bit
   A underrated.   B overrated.   C indispensable.
3. The new banking laws have
   A had big benefits for us.   B made big benefits for us.
   C benefit us.
4. All this technology isn't really necessary. We
   A can't do without it.   B can do without.
   C can do without it.
5. The new measures have made a big difference at work. This manager has been
   A forced for good.   B a force of good.
   C a force for good.
6. That building is hideous and it serves no purpose. What
   A a space waste!   B a waste of space!
   C a waster of space!

Continuous aspect

3 Match the sentence halves.

1. 1 We've built a tree house, which ☐
   2 We've been building a tree house which ☐
   A we're hoping to finish tomorrow.
   B the children play in every day.
2. 1 He might have been voting ☐
   2 He might have voted ☐
   A this morning, which would explain why he wasn't here.
   B for the Green Party in the last election, but I doubt it.
3. 1 Dana was being taught Russian ☐
   2 Dana was taught Russian ☐
   A the last time I saw her.
   B when she was a child.
4. 1 We'll have been studying ☐
   2 We'll have studied ☐
   A the Present Perfect six times if we do this lesson.
   B here for exactly fifteen years by this time on Monday.
5. 1 It's raining ☐
   2 It rains ☐
   A between June and September.
   B again.
6. 1 I've been seeing her ☐
   2 I've seen her ☐
   A in the same place at the same convention every year since 1982!
   B before.

66

Fronting

4 Rewrite the sentences using 'fronting' expressions and the words in brackets.

1. I'm fed up with all that noise. (thing/irritates)
2. My main concern is the cost involved. (what/worries)
3. To tell the truth, I'm tired of this game. (fact, matter)
4. If we open the shop on Sundays, that could be a solution. (what/work/if)
5. There are too many people; that's the problem. (trouble/is)
6. He broke his promise. There's nothing we can do to change that. (fact/remains)
7. We should have eaten earlier. (What/needed/have/done)
8. The house is in good condition. That's the important thing. (point)

Vocabulary

5 Find and correct the mistakes.

1. A: This toaster keeps to burn the toast.
   B: Well, why don't you buy a new one?
2. A: I can't get this door to close. Can you help me?
   B: Let me to see.
3. A: Can you give me a hand tomorrow? I'm having problems finishing all this work.
   B: I'd have to think of that. I'm pretty busy myself.
4. A: She's always late. How can we make her turn up on time?
   B: That's a trick question.
5. A: My car can't start. What can I do?
   B: That's a difficult question.
6. A: This drawer seems to be too stuck. How does it open?
   B: That's a good question.

6 Six of the lines have an extra word. Write the extra words and tick (✓) the correct sentences.

1. Behaviourist theory has its own roots in an experiment by Ivan Pavlov. _____
2. His research was to have far-reaching and consequences for psychology. _____
3. When Pavlov placed meat powder on a dog's tongue, the dog salivated. _____
4. Pavlov then began ringing a bell just before giving the dog the meat powder. _____
5. This resulted but in the dog salivating when it heard the bell, even if it _____
6. didn't get any meat powder afterwards. Many psychologists concluded that by _____
7. a major source of motivation is conditioning. This had a huge influence so _____
8. on many areas of life, including language learning. For example, _____
9. behaviourist theory gave a rise to the audiolingual method (listen and repeat). _____
10. It also brought us about many changes in the teaching materials used. _____

7 Complete the crossword.

Across
1. however
2. with reference to
3. in order of first letter (in _____ order)
4. suggest (a fact) without stating it overtly
5. produce (e.g. ideas)
6. build (e.g. an argument)
7. emphasise (maybe in writing)

Down
8. consecutively (for three days _____)
9. to sum up (in _____)
10. also (what's _____)
11. in order of which came first (in _____ order)
12. to test/judge
13. to be specific (to be _____)
14. also (in _____) (formal)

9.1 Vision

Vocabulary | the arts

1 Complete the word cross and find the key word. Look on page 117 of the Students' Book to help you.

1 It was funny to watch although the acting was really _____ .
2 The Mona Lisa is an _____ .
3 It was a beautiful opera and the scenery was just _____ .
4 The town is full of _____ architecture.
5 The artist's _____ of the royal family are well-known.
6 The special effects in the new *Star Wars* film are _____ .
7 It's a long book about the history of nuclear physics, so it's quite a _____ read.
8 Unfortunately the characters are rather _____ .
9 I'm really into _____ art at the moment.

Grammar | dependent prepositions

2 Choose the correct prepositions. Who is the artist?

Perhaps one of the most tragic masters of art, this painter yearned (1) *for/on/to* recognition during his lifetime, but was denied it until after his death. He is universally seen as one of the greatest artists (2) *at/in/of* all time.
(3) *To/On/For* one occasion, he said of his paintings: 'I cannot help it if my paintings do not sell. But the time will come when people will realise that they are worth more than the cost of the paint.' His vision was correct. This artist was an indisputable genius, who was also undeniably ignored. He became famous (4) *for/of/at* the hundreds of bold, bright paintings he produced, many of which have become some of the best known, popularised paintings of the twentieth century, but only one of which was ever sold during his lifetime. He drew inspiration (5) *for/by/from* the places where he lived and worked, and also from the people he enjoyed relationships (6) *with/in/on*. However, the work he specialised (7) *at/in/on* was avant-garde (8) *in/for/of* his time, and as such, was not accepted by the general public.
He spent the latter part of his life absorbed (9) *in/on/at* his work. However, he was always (10) *over/in/under* stress, and suffered (11) *for/from/of* depression. It is now thought that epilepsy may have contributed (12) *to/with/in* the psychological breakdowns which plagued him until his untimely death.

How to … | express certainty and uncertainty

3 Rewrite the sentences using the words in CAPITALS.

1 He was certainly one of the greatest musicians of all time. DOUBT
2 We are not entirely sure where he was born. CERTAIN
3 There is no question that the theory was wrong. UNDENIABLY
4 There are doubts about the premises on which he based his theories. QUESTIONABLE
5 There is no argument about the fact that the damage was caused by the car. IRREFUTABLE
6 We are not certain which driver is responsible for the accident. CLEAR-CUT
7 We cannot be sure but eating small amounts of chocolate may have beneficial health properties. DEBATABLE
8 We can be certain that smoking tobacco limits your life expectancy. INDISPUTABLE

Reading

4 a Read the short biography on page 69 and choose the correct answers.

1 Why is Stephen Hawking so famous?
   A Because he has researched time travel.
   B Because of his ideas and his physical condition.
   C Because he appeared on TV shows like *The Simpsons*.
2 Stephen suffers from a motor neurone disease which
   A has left him in a vegetative state.
   B means he can talk unaided but he cannot move.
   C makes both speech and movement almost impossible.
3 His physical condition has
   A meant that he never enjoyed a family life.
   B probably contributed to his fame.
   C impeded him from achieving greatness in his professional career.

How Stephen Hawking discovered how time began.

(1) Stephen Hawking is arguably Britain's most important scientist and undoubtedly the most famous – a man who has transcended ordinary fame to become a cultural icon. Few scientists have been so revered, and appearances on TV shows like *Star Trek* and *The Simpsons* only add to the mystique. Part of the fascination, of course, stems from his disability. Afflicted with a rare illness called amyotrophic lateral sclerosis (ALS), a type of motor neurone disease, he is unable to talk or move almost any part of his body. Slumped in a wheelchair and communicating only through his computer-generated voice, Hawking is the embodiment of a pre-eminent mind pondering the nature of space and time while trapped in a crippled frame.

(2) But it wasn't always like this. There was a time when Hawking could walk and talk unaided, a time when he was just beginning to formulate his groundbreaking ideas on the universe.

(3) Stephen William Hawking was born in Oxford, England, on 8th January 1942 (exactly 300 years after the death of astronomer Galileo Galilei). His parents' house was in north London, but during the Second World War Oxford was considered a safer place to bring up children. When he was eight years old his family moved to St Albans, a town about twenty miles north of London, where he went to school. And in 1959 Stephen followed his father's footsteps by going to University College, Oxford. Stephen wanted to study mathematics, although his father would have preferred him to study medicine. But mathematics was not available at University College, so he did physics instead. After three years and not very much work he was awarded a first class honours degree in natural science.

(4) Stephen then went on to Cambridge to do research in cosmology, there being no-one working in that area in Oxford at the time. Tragedy struck, however, in 1963, when he was diagnosed with ALS and given only two years to live. But Hawking was determined to have both a family life and a career. In July 1965 he married Jane Wilde. The couple had been introduced after his grave diagnosis, at a New Year's Eve party in St Albans. In 1967 the couple's first child, Robert, was born. Two other children, Lucy and Timothy, followed.

(5) While ALS ravaged Hawking's body, his mind soared higher. As he wrote in *The Brief History of Time*: 'One evening in 1970, I started to think about black holes as I was getting into bed. My disability makes this a rather slow process so I had plenty of time to think.' It was these musings that led to his most famous discovery.

(6) In 1974 Hawking unveiled his radical theory of black hole explosions, and in 1979 he was appointed Lucasian Professor of Mathematics at Cambridge, a post held in 1669 by Sir Isaac Newton. Hawking was just thirty-seven years old.

(7) Professional glory wasn't enough for Hawking, though. By 1985 medical bills were draining his academic salary. So Hawking conceived a popular science book, the proceeds from which could pay for his round-the-clock care. *A Brief History of Time* was published by Bantum Press and went on to sell over ten million copies worldwide.

(8) From then on he became a household name, but Hawking still surprises those who know only his public image. He relishes driving fast around Cambridge in his wheelchair, despite being hit by a car in 1991. Eyebrows rose when he left Jane for his former nurse, Elaine Mason, whom he married in 1995. And later newspapers had a field day when he was seen enjoying the company of ladies in Stringfellows nightclub, in London.

(9) In recent years, Hawking has turned his mind to time travel. In the 1990s he came up with a theory that explains why travelling back in time isn't possible. Since nobody has yet built a time machine, there's no telling whether he's right. But there's no doubt that Hawking's own place in history is already assured.

---

b Find words and phrases in the text that mean:

1. much admired (*adj*) (para 1) _____
2. the best of its kind (*adj*) (para 1) _____
3. new and radically different (discoveries/research, etc.) (*adj*) (para 2) _____
4. serious or bad (*adj*) (para 4) _____
5. thoughts (*n*) (para 5) _____
6. enjoys great pleasure from (*v*) (para 8) _____
7. there is no way of knowing (para 9) _____
8. certain (*adj*) (para 9) _____

c Find and correct the mistakes.

Hawking was born in London exactly 300 years after the astronomer Galileo. He went to university in Oxford to study mathematics, and later went on to do research at Cambridge, where he became a professor. In 1963 he was diagnosed with a rare motor neurone disease and told he had only a short time to live. The disease left him severely disabled and unable to have children. Fortunately, he had no financial worries as he was able to continue working at the university. He later published an academic science book about his ideas on the universe.

9.2

Vocabulary | describing art

1 Put the letters in brackets in the correct order to make words to complete the sentences.

1 I like _____ paintings best, especially ones by artists like Kandinsky and Miró. (scatbart)
2 It's very _____ . You can't help but notice it when you walk into the room. (tigrnski)
3 His techniques were very _____ for the time. (navat-draeg)
4 Her still life paintings are _____ and simple. (lanpi)
5 The landscapes are very _____ and relaxing to look at. (nailqurt)
6 He is famous for his _____ portraits. (lourcoluf)
7 I found the sculptures of dead animals highly _____ . (tirgsubind)
8 It's a masterpiece. Absolutely _____ ! (nungisnt)
9 Their earlier works were more _____ in style. (ladanotirit)
10 Some people love them, but personally I find landscapes rather _____ . (ludl)

How to ... | say what you like/dislike

2 Complete the mini-dialogues by adding words from the box.

> my   admired   into   all-time
> relate   fan   cup   kind

1 A: Did you like the dress?
   B: I'm afraid it's just not my of thing at all.
2 A: What do you think of the decor?
   B: It's really not taste.
3 A: Did you enjoy Imogen's latest exhibition?
   B: Yes. I'm really her work.
4 A: How about this one? Do you like the style?
   B: It's not really my of tea.
5 A: Have you heard the new James Blunt album?
   B: I'm not a big of his stuff.
6 A: *The Big Chill* is on TV tonight.
   B: Brilliant. It's one of my favourites.
7 A: Ali Smith won an award for her latest novel.
   B: She deserved to. I've always her work.
8 A: What do you think of the exhibition?
   B: I just can't to this kind of thing.

Grammar | discourse markers

3 Use the words in CAPITALS to complete the sentences with discourse markers.

_____ , I'm going to talk to you about education. SAYING

As I was saying, I'm going to talk to you about education.

1 There's been some _____ misunderstanding. KIND
2 I can _____ see what you mean. SORT
3 _____ , I haven't really understood a word you are talking about. HONEST
4 _____ , I would rather stay at home and watch a film. TRUTH
5 We can _____ be sure of their intention to purchase. MORE
6 _____ , we should be able to get a good price. RATE
7 _____ , I wouldn't want to stay there on my own. MIND
8 _____ , I think the ideas should be discussed at a meeting. MATTER/FACT
9 _____ , it is the best offer we are going to get. FAR/CONCERNED
10 _____ when we should leave, I don't think it makes any difference. FOR
11 _____ , they proved us wrong in the end. FACT
12 _____ changing the policy completely, I'm not in a position to answer. REGARDS

Vocabulary | crime

4 Complete the sentences using words from the box.

> hideout   stuffed   haul   crack   undercover
> chainsaw   tracked   mastermind

1 He is suspected of being the _____ behind the bombings.
2 The man was discovered in a _____ in the woods.
3 He worked _____ in Germany and Northern Ireland.
4 Detectives finally _____ her down in California.
5 She quickly _____ two more sweaters into her bag.
6 They used a _____ to cut through the heavy doors.
7 This new evidence could help detectives to _____ the case.
8 The gang escaped with a _____ worth hundreds of pounds.

Reading

5 a Read the extract and choose the best title.
1. A Good Deal
2. Momentarily Fooled
3. Texan Rebel

1 In 1952, Elmyr de Hory returned to Los Angeles after a prosperous sojourn to Dallas, Texas. He had managed to sell some of his stash of alleged masterpieces, including some Picasso and Matisse drawings. He had made a huge profit and was hoping he would be equally successful in Southern California. Elmyr had set up an appointment with art dealer Frank Perls, owner of a well-known Beverly Hills gallery, and he planned to unload more of his art works for another sizeable profit.

2 Elmyr dressed in his best suit for the occasion, carrying with him a large portfolio. At his meeting with Perls, Elmyr presented what he claimed were drawings he'd inherited from his family following World War II. The portfolio purportedly included sketches from Picasso, Matisse, Renoir and Modigliani.

3 Perls took one look at the works and was immensely impressed. After all, it's not often that one has the chance to hold great masterpieces by some of the world's most famous artists. However, the longer Perls looked at the pictures the more concerned he became. It was clear that something was wrong and Perls' worrisome expression discomforted Elymr.

4 According to Clifford Irving's book *Fake!* Perls questioned Elmyr about his address and other detailed personal information, causing Elmyr to become nervous. Perls then calmly placed the pictures back into the portfolio, tied the strings, and then suddenly threw them at Elmyr. Elmyr was shocked by the unexpected action and was uncertain what to do next until Perls ordered him to get out.

5 Elmyr then walked out of the gallery with Perls yelling behind him. Perls observed what an untrained eye would likely never notice: these works were fakes. It was also true that they were created masterfully.

6 To Perls' surprise, Elmyr asked him, after being thrown out of the gallery, whether he thought the drawings were well done. According to Irving, Perls replied: 'They certainly fooled me for a few minutes,' before ordering the counterfeiter away again. The incident was not Elmyr's first or last time at trying to sell excellent forgeries. In fact, he had been doing it successfully for years.

7 Unbeknown to Frank Perls, Elmyr had sold some forgeries to Perls' brother Klaus in New York several years earlier. Elmyr's involvement with the two Perls brothers would later cause unexpected problems. In fact, one of the Perls brothers would be directly involved in what would later be the end of Elmyr's career as a skillful art forger.

8 For approximately three decades Elmyr de Hory used his extraordinary talent to reproduce masterpieces from some of the world's greatest artists, including Picasso, Vlaminck, Chagall, Toulouse-Lautrec, Dufy, Derain, Matisse, Degas, Bonnard, Laurencin and Modigliani. His accuracy for detail fooled even the most skilled art connoisseurs into believing that his creations were authentic. Given their alleged provenance, Elmyr's sold his forgeries for high prices. Moreover, he managed to elude Interpol and the FBI for most of his criminal career.

9 Elmyr de Hory eventually became known worldwide as one of the most talented art forgers in history. Even after his death, Elmyr's works still attracted attention. Some of them even sold for the same prices as the originals. Like many famous painters, however, he would die penniless after a series of unfortunate events.

b Read the story again. Mark the statements true (T) or false (F).
1. Elmyr de Hory travelled to Dallas with just a couple of paintings. ☐
2. He sold paintings for a small profit to art dealers. ☐
3. Perls immediately spotted Elmyr as a fake by the way he was dressed. ☐
4. Elmyr made up stories about the origins of the paintings. ☐
5. Perls' questions worried Elmyr. ☐
6. Elmyr had been successfully selling fake paintings for about thirty years. ☐
7. He had been chased constantly by the FBI and Interpol. ☐
8. During his life Elmyr's paintings sold for large sums of money, but after his death, they quickly lost their value. ☐

c Work out the meaning of the words 1–8. Use the context of the story to help you.
1. prosperous (para 1) _____
2. stash (para 1) _____
3. purportedly (para 2) _____
4. worrisome (para 3) _____
5. masterfully (para 5) _____
6. forgeries (para 7) _____
7. fooled (para 8) _____
8. elude (para 8) _____

9.3

Vocabulary | cameras and photos

1 Complete the dialogue using words from the box.

> close-up   out of focus   disposable
> foreground   accessories   flash
> digital   holiday snaps

Julia: Do you want to come and see my (1) _____ of Greece and Turkey?
Daphne: Sure.
Julia: That's me in the (2) _____ . Behind me is the Acropolis. This one's a bit (3) _____ . You can't see it very clearly.
Daphne: But most of these are great pictures. Did you use a (4) _____ camera?
Julia: No, just a cheap little (5) _____ camera. I threw it away after the holiday.
Daphne: So it didn't have any (6) _____ like a tripod or anything?
Julia: No way! I prefer to keep it simple. This one's a bit dark. We took it at night and I don't think the (7) _____ was working.
Daphne: Wow! Who's this, taking up the whole frame?!
Julia: This is a (8) _____ of my aunt. You can see every pore in her skin!

Grammar | unreal past

2 Match the sentence halves.
1. He wishes ☐
2. I wish I hadn't ☐
3. I wish I ☐
4. If only they ☐
5. It's about ☐
6. It's high time ☐
7. They'd sooner see ☐
8. I'd rather you didn't put ☐
9. What if you hadn't ☐
10. Supposing I could ☐

a time you had a haircut.
b your feet on the furniture.
c been wearing a seat belt?
d were here now.
e offer you a bonus?
f we had a little talk.
g you than her.
h bought that car.
i could play the guitar.
j you would stop singing.

3 Rewrite the sentences using the words in brackets.
1 Rashid lost his passport so he couldn't board the plane. (only)
  If _____ .
2 You're acting like a child and you should stop! (high)
  It's _____ .
3 For me, the best option would have been to take the train. (sooner)
  I _____ .
4 We really should get back to work now. (about)
  It's _____ .
5 Can you imagine being offered that job? Would you accept? (if)
  What _____ ?
6 What will happen if we press this button? (supposing)
  _____ ?
7 Phyllis is an only child but she wants a baby sister. (wish)
  Phyllis _____ .
8 What did you want to do last night: go out or watch a DVD? (rather)
  Would _____ ?

How to … | respond to hypothetical questions

4 Put the words in the correct order to make responses to the questions.
1 What if the board asked you to become Chairman of the company?
  it's agree highly I'd likely
2 Supposing they stopped you illegally? What would you do?
  I taking consider them court definitely to would
3 If she asked you, would you lend her ten thousand pounds?
  it's to I'd able be that do unlikely that
4 You're not thinking of quitting the course, are you?
  there's I do way that would no
5 What if we offered you half of our winnings?
  I agree probably that to would
6 Would you be willing to coach the team for free?
  I that I might suppose doing consider

Listening

5 a 9.1 Cover the tapescript. Listen to an interview with a photographer. Answer the questions.

1. How did her family influence her choice of career?
2. What did she like about her first camera?
3. Why does she take different types of photo?
4. What type of pictures is she taking at the moment?
5. What 'has its own sort of visual vocabulary' and what do you think she means by this?

b Complete the summary with one word in each space. Listen again to check.

Sandrine started by taking photos of _____ in her _____ garden at the age of _____ . She now photographs many things, including nature and famous _____ . She thinks a photographer's job is to capture _____ and _____ . She says she is interested in _____ . Sandrine lives near a _____ and loves the light there.

c Look at the tapescript. Find phrases 1–8. Match them to definitions a–h.

1. what marks you out ☐
2. your incredibly diverse output ☐
3. a restless soul ☐
4. being pigeonholed ☐
5. feeling a bit peeved ☐
6. at the end of the lens ☐
7. every subject under the sun ☐
8. a sense of awe ☐

a. as the subject of a photo
b. being forced to fit into a category
c. what makes you different
d. all the topics that exist
e. a feeling of wonder because something is amazing or beyond normal life
f. someone who can't stay still or stay in the same place
g. feeling annoyed
h. the things you produce are in a very wide range of styles

TAPESCRIPT

I: Sandrine, can you tell us a bit about how you got started as a photographer?

S: It all goes back to my grandmother, actually. She lived in Colombia as a child, and when she moved back to England she insisted on planting tropical flowers in this tiny back garden of hers because they reminded her of her childhood. Whenever the flowers bloomed of course, the colours were astonishing. Now, on my tenth birthday my father gave me a Polaroid and I started taking pictures of grandma's garden. And the beauty of the Polaroid was that you didn't have to send the pictures away to be developed. They just slipped out of the bottom of the camera in all their glory.

I: From pictures of grandma's garden to celebrities, landscape, underwater photography and even social realism. What marks you out is your incredibly diverse output. The product of a restless soul perhaps?

S: You could say that. I dislike being pigeonholed. I remember reading an article about contemporary photographers a few years ago, which described me as 'Sandrine Kafer, the celebrity photographer', and I remember feeling a bit peeved that that was how some journalist saw me. I'd always thought of myself as a photographer pure and simple, whose job is to capture a moment of truth and beauty, and whether it's a famous person at the end of the lens or two little boys on a bicycle or soldiers or life at the bottom of the ocean, in many ways it's the same thing to me.

I: So this diversity hasn't been a conscious career decision? It's something …

S: Not really, no. I just take opportunities where I find them, and I suppose, above all, I'm interested in everything. I have a library of about 6000 books at home, very few of them on photography, and they cover every subject under the sun. And once you start getting interested in something you want to see it and find the truth in it, and then, of course, if you're a photographer, you want to capture it on film.

I: Your recent work seems less crowded, perhaps more tranquil than anything you've done before.

S: It may be my age! No, I live on twenty acres of land with a river close by and birds and animals. The light is stunning, and it always amazes me that the river can look like this at five in the morning and like that at midday and different again at dusk. Actually, whenever you work with water, there is a sense of awe. It's where life began. It has its own rhythm and its own sort of visual vocabulary.

I: Above all in your work we perhaps see …

Review and consolidation unit 9

Dependent prepositions

1 a Add the correct prepositions.

1. devoted his life _____
2. the development _____
3. _____ the field (e.g. of physics)
4. suffer _____ (something)
5. immersed _____
6. specialises _____
7. _____ pressure
8. succeed _____
9. _____ several occasions
10. in recognition _____
11. draw inspiration _____
12. (one of the best) _____ all time

b Read the letter. Replace the phrases in *italics* with the prepositional phrases in Ex. 1a.

Discourse markers

2 Ten words are missing. Add them to complete the mini-dialogues.

1. **A:** Didn't you just love that film?
   B: As matter of fact, we found it rather boring.
2. **A:** Be honest, I don't like ballet much.
   B: Far as the skill is concerned I think it's wonderful, but I can't say I've seen much of it.
3. **A:** Isn't that CD brilliant?
   B: To tell you truth, I think it's a bit overrated.
4. **A:** That film was kind long, wasn't it?
   B: Long? I fell asleep at least twice. It was endless!
5. **A:** Bye, Tom! Anyway, Mary, I was saying, that restaurant is fantastic.
   B: Mind, it's not exactly cheap.
6. **A:** So if you can get three tickets that'd be great.
   B: Any rate, I'll get at least two, OK?
7. **A:** He wrote, directed and starred in that play.
   B: Frankly, he more less did everything!
8. **A:** Sorry, Keith. I interrupted you.
   B: I was going to say was that I enjoyed the exhibition very much.

Hi Arline,

How are you? Everything's fine here at Los Alamos. You wouldn't believe some of the scientists I'm working with. There's Hans Vogel, who **is focussing on** particle theory. He has really **given everything of himself to** his research. He's probably one of the greatest scientists **in history**. There's also Bernheimer, who won the Nobel Prize **due to** his contribution to our understanding of nanotechnology. He's the world's greatest expert **in his area**. He is totally **focussed on** his work, which is **the creation and production of** a new type of weapon. I've managed to speak to him **a few times**, and even though he's working **in very tough conditions**, he doesn't seem to **feel the** stress.

I've been able to **get motivated through my contact with** these people and I really hope I can **do well** in my work here.

Love,

Richard

Unreal past | wish/If only

3 Read the text. Underline the best words to complete it.

Most companies, on making a mistake, publicly deny it and privately say, 'Oh no! If only we (1) *have/had/should have* done this!' Venture capitalists, who help fund new businesses, spend half their lives wishing they (2) *have poured/must have put/had poured* money into one thing and not another. Not Bessemer Venture Partners. This company has an 'anti-portfolio' web site which lists the great opportunities they missed. The list contains some of the biggest names in business. (3) *If only/Should/What if* Bessemer had put money into unknown company, Apple Computers? (4) *Supposing/Supposed/Wishing* they hadn't turned down eBay? At the time eBay sold stamps and comic books, and Bessemer didn't see the potential. If only they (5) *must have been/had been/had be* able to read the future! Bessemer also turned down Google before it was famous. So why does Bessemer admit these mistakes? According to the website, they (6) *would sooner/are sooner/sooner* laugh at their errors than try to cover them up. It may also be a marketing ploy: new businesses (7) *had rather/prefer/would rather* go to a venture company which has a reputation for honesty and openness than one that doesn't. Our conclusion? It's (8) *the right time/high time/the time* other companies came out and admitted (or even laughed at) their own mistakes.

Vocabulary

4 Put the letters in **bold** in the correct order to make words to complete the text.

Jackson Pollock's early paintings were (1) **fgitareivu**, though never realistic. In the 1940s his work became more (2) **asttacrb** and less (3) **tdaanilorit** until he reached his zenith in the drip paintings of the mid forties. These were truly (4) **vatan-rgdae**, (5) **stgninnu** works, painted on a huge scale. Although critics called Pollock a barbarian because of his technique, and found the violence of both his life and work (6) **dibgsrniut**, what is (7) **stgrniki** about Hans Namuth's film of him painting is that he seems completely (8) **tqnaiurl** as he dances around the canvas, dripping paint. After 1951 Pollock did a number of (9) **moehrocnom** paintings and his work became less (10) **crouulolf**.

5 Complete the sentences using the words in brackets.
1. We were able to _____ a number of patients, but we couldn't _____ that the theory was correct. (prove/test)
2. After giving me the _____ to teach, he told me there was a _____ that the course would be cancelled. (opportunity/possibility)
3. There's a _____ in that company because one of the employees is on _____ . (vacation/vacancy)
4. Baggy trousers don't really _____ me, but I can't _____ those tight ones. (fit into/suit)
5. All those who _____ the seminar will be asked to _____ at the conference. (assist/attended)
6. I'm not doing anything _____ , but tomorrow I'm leaving. No, not tomorrow, on Monday _____ . (at the moment/actually)
7. We had a school _____ and had a _____ to discuss how we could help the school financially. (reunion/meeting)
8. It seemed proper and _____ to make rules related to _____ issues such as racism and sexism. (sensible/sensitive)

6 Cross out the ending that is NOT possible.
1. That type of art isn't
   A my kind of thing. B my cup of tea.
   C my liking.
2. It became clear that the facts in the case were
   A indisputable. B without a doubt.
   C undeniable.
3. Bearing in mind the circumstances, I
   A would consider to do that.
   B would agree to that.
   C suppose I might agree.
4. That's what they say, but in my opinion, it's
   A questionable. B debatable.
   C unquestionably.
5. People think he reached the North Pole, but it's not
   A 100 percent certain. B without a doubt.
   C clear-cut.
6. Her paintings weren't universally popular, but the critic Herman Bowers was
   A a big favourite. B a big fan.
   C really into her work.
7. Daniel is worried that I'm going to leave the company, but
   A there's no way I'd do that.
   B I wouldn't probably do that.
   C it's unlikely I'd be able to do that.
8. Some people hated those art-house movies, but Mrs Williams
   A really related to that type of thing.
   B had always admired them.
   C couldn't agree to them.

75

10.1 Feelings

Listening and Vocabulary

1. **10.1** Cover the tapescript. Listen and write sentences to describe how each speaker is feeling, and why. Use phrases from the box.

   > in two minds   down in the dumps
   > over the moon   at her wits end   wound up

   Speaker 1: _____

   Speaker 2: _____

   Speaker 3: _____

   Speaker 4: _____

   Speaker 5: _____

2. Listen again. Write the number of the speaker next to each expression.

1	It is the most amazing feeling.	Speaker ____
2	It is so annoying.	Speaker ____
3	I can't believe how happy I am.	Speaker ____
4	It makes me so angry.	Speaker ____
5	I don't know if it's worth it.	Speaker ____
6	I'm just a bit fed up.	Speaker ____
7	I'm worried sick.	Speaker ____
8	I can't help thinking that something must've happened.	Speaker ____
9	I don't feel I'm really making the most of life.	Speaker ____
10	I'm just so excited.	Speaker ____

TAPESCRIPT

1
I'm just a bit fed up, I think. I'm not really enjoying my job at the moment, and I don't seem to have much time to go out either, so I don't feel I'm really making the most of life. I often don't get home until late, and it's too late to cook so I usually end up just eating cereal in front of the TV and then falling asleep. And then before I know it, it's time to go back to work again and ...

2
I can't understand why she hasn't called me yet. I mean she said she would call as soon as she arrived, and it's been two days now. I can't help thinking that something must've happened. It's so not like her, I mean not to send even a text message. I'm worried sick. I'm going to have to call the police and ask if anyone has reported ...

3
Yes, it's a boy. We went to have the tests yesterday, and I'm just so excited. I can't believe you can actually see the baby on the screen, with his little hands and feet and everything. I've got a photo of him, and it is the most amazing feeling. I can't believe how happy I am, and to think that in just a few months time ...

4
I can't believe it. It is so annoying. I have waited all this time to get an appointment, months and months, and now they write a letter to say that they can't treat me in that hospital anyway, and I need to go somewhere else. I mean why didn't they just say that before, six months ago?! We pay huge amounts of money into the system and it makes me so angry when you can't even get a simple doctor's appointment ...

5
Oh, I'm really not sure. I could come just for the day, I suppose, but it's such a long journey that I don't know if it's worth it to drive all that way, and then not be able to stay for longer. On the other hand, it would be great to see you all again, and if I don't come now, I don't know when I'll next have the chance. And it's been ages since ...

Grammar | modals

3 Rewrite the sentences using the words in brackets.

1 It wasn't really necessary for us to bring all this equipment. (need)
   _____
2 There is a good chance that they'll find out sooner or later. (bound)
   _____
3 I think it would be a good idea if we looked around the house first. (ought)
   _____
4 She will probably do well in the marathon. (likely)
   _____
5 I can't believe there is no easier way to do this. (must)
   _____
6 I've asked her a hundred times already but she is refusing to change her position. (won't)
   _____
7 It's impossible for them to charge that much for a service. It's ridiculous. (can't)
   _____
8 It's likely that we'll bump into you at the party on Saturday. (might)
   _____
9 They ask you to take your shoes off before you go in. (supposed)
   _____
10 It's going to take a few months before we can move to the new premises. (will)
   _____

4 Choose the correct words to complete the sentences.

1 Tim's flight took over fifteen hours.
  He _____ be exhausted.
  A is supposed to   B is likely   C must
2 If you don't speak Mandarin, you _____ accept the job.
  A can't   B are supposed   C are bound
3 Nobody _____ to talk in the library.
  A is bound   B is supposed   C can't
4 He's had the problem for weeks, but he _____ see a doctor.
  A ought   B won't   C is likely
5 The accommodation office _____ to help you find somewhere to live.
  A ought   B can't   C might
6 You didn't _____ to have it delivered. I could have picked it up myself.
  A ought   B might   C need

Vocabulary | idioms

5 Complete the text using phrases from the box.

> chances of success in life seemed slim
> dwell   gut feelings and hunches
> look on the bright side
> open to new experiences
> work out well in the long run
> getting the things we really want out of life
> boost your intuition   tendency

New life course

Life for many of us has evolved to the point where we find ourselves stuck with few perceived choices. Life is stressful when we find ourselves unsatisfied with the way we feel, doing things too much of the time that we don't really want to do, and not (1) _____. We have a (2) _____ to (3) _____ on our problems rather than seek out new solutions for the future.

But life doesn't have to be like this. There can be a better way, a way that will help you to (4) _____.

You can create a new life. A life revised in small but crucial ways – or perhaps you will totally change the way things have been up to now. You choose, of course. But first you need to know just who you really are and to shed the conditioning imposed on you by decades of conforming to other peoples' expectations and other peoples' interpretations. Before, your (5) _____. Now is the time to change all that.

It is possible to find out what your true goals in life are and to attain those goals. It is possible to (6) _____ and learn to follow your (7) _____ without being afraid of the consequences. It is possible to effectively manage anxiety, stress, anger and other painful emotions, and to make the best of your time. It is possible to recognise what your problems really are and to fix those problems for good. With the right knowledge, you can achieve the outcomes you desire. You will be (8) _____, and as a result, unlimited possibilities open up for you. This course provides the knowledge you need to help things (9) _____.

10.2

Grammar | modals of deduction

1 Rewrite the sentences using the words in CAPITALS.

1. It's impossible for it to have been Pete who you saw. CAN'T
2. There is no answer. Perhaps they have gone to bed. COULD
3. You weren't looking where you were going. The car nearly killed you. MIGHT
4. I'm not sure that they're still in the city. I think they moved. MAY
5. I'm glad you came. It would have been impossible without you. COULDN'T
6. I can't find it anywhere, but I know it's here. MUST
7. Rick and June are undecided about whether to come to the wedding reception. MIGHT
8. Someone called and left a message. It's possible that it was Kate. MAY
9. I can't believe you are being serious. MUST
10. They are still not here. Perhaps they got lost. MIGHT

Vocabulary | strong adjectives of feeling

2 Put the letters in brackets in the correct order to make adjectives to complete the sentences.

1. He was _____ about being asked to play in the band. (ldrihtel)
2. Her family are _____ about her name being published in the press. (soruifu)
3. Emma was somewhat _____ by his directness. (kante bacak)
4. The crowd lining the streets were _____ when they caught sight of the celebrities. (citsceta)
5. Sarah was absolutely _____ to him, and it hurt. (dirntfenief)
6. She's been so _____ since Patrick left him. (silermabe)
7. He's really _____ about passing the exam! (fcudfeh)
8. He was _____ in politics. (terenuetinsd)
9. Sid is _____ of heights. (frerietid)
10. When I found out how much money we'd made, I was absolutely _____ . (blastabfredge)
11. When we heard the news we were _____ . (scmurktudb)
12. Customers were _____ by the price increases. (tuadroge)
13. Sandy will be _____ to see you. (lehtdideg)
14. She was absolutely _____ that he had lied. (divil)
15. I'm _____ of spiders. (diterfipe)
16. She was really _____ about the way her father treated her. (spute)

Reading

3 a Read the text. Tick (✓) the feelings and emotions that are described.

excitement ☐   pity ☐
frustration ☐   fear ☐
ecstasy ☐   jealousy ☐
hurt ☐   regret ☐
contentment ☐   surprise ☐

b Which part of the text refers to each emotion?

What I've learned about husbands

1. When Lady Sarah Graham Moon chopped up her husband's suits she became a heroine for spurned spouses. Then she found happiness, but it was not to last, she tells Giles Hattersley

2. It took Lady Sarah Graham Moon two marriages, five sons, and one very famous act of revenge to find the perfect man. After sixty years spent suffocating in the upper classes, she found a man who was not interested in class differences or money. She moved David Denyer, a local gamekeeper, into the house and together the pair raised chickens and gun dogs. For the first time in her life she was happy.

3. In February she found him dying by the back door. 'Just there,' she says, pointing to a spot beyond a jumble of boots and wax jackets. 'I found him on his back, lying on top of a gun. He was obsessed with the jackdaws in the roof and kept a gun to hand so he could have a shot at them. He died quietly with his head in my lap. One tiny wound and no blood. His final word was "Gun".'

4 Although her eyes are moist, the sixty-eight-year-old's voice remains brisk and unfussy throughout this, her first interview since the tragedy. Ladies from this part of the countryside don't do excess emotion.

5 'Death is all around,' she booms. 'We shoot dogs and we kill rabbits. Of course it isn't very nice but there's no use crying great crocodile tears. When David died I didn't go into hysterics or rush down to the hospital to see his body. He's dead and that's that.'

6 Her no-fuss attitude should not surprise you. Moon and drama are old friends. Today she sits grandly on an antique armchair, surrounded by dog portraits and stuffed birds, but it was with similar pragmatism that, fourteen years ago, she became notorious for wreaking terrible revenge.

7 When her second marriage to Sir Peter Graham Moon crumbled, he moved a younger woman ('Not that much younger,' sniffs Moon) into the couple's Berkshire village. When he failed to turn up to see his wife one day, she calmly snipped the sleeves off thirty-two of his Savile Row suits, trashed his BMW with a can of white paint and deposited rare wines from his cellar on doorsteps around the village like a milkman.

8 Moon became an instant media star. She had a column in *The Sun*, wrote a book, set up the Old Bags Club for other abandoned wives, and was even asked on the Oprah Winfrey Show. ('I think Oprah expected me to cry or something,' she snorts. 'She asked me if I wanted a hug. I said, 'Get away from me. I'm English'.')

9 Always ready with a quick answer, she was the spokeswoman for revenge, but in reality she says what drove her to act the way she did was not the need for revenge. 'At the time everybody put my actions down to feminist retribution and jealousy, but it wasn't like that at all,' she says. 'It was sheer terror.'

10 Last month an inquest returned an open verdict on Denyer's death after a firearms expert all but ruled out the possibility of it being an accident. The court heard how the seventy-one-year-old's knees were wrecked with arthritis and he had become depressed with a worsening heart condition. Coupled with his excellent knowledge of guns (he had ten), it was suggested that suicide was the likely cause. Moon strongly disagrees.

11 'If David had wanted to kill himself he would have done it properly,' she says, holding an imaginary rifle to her chin. 'He wouldn't have made a bad shot like that, and he wouldn't have done it two feet from the back door. I imagine he picked up the gun by the barrel and tripped with his bad knees.'

12 And now she is on her own again? 'Oh don't be depressing,' she thunders. 'At least he left me feeling more confident than the last one did. David asked me to marry him, you know, but I said no. I thought two bad ones was quite enough.'

13 Do you regret it now? 'Yes,' she says, surprising herself. 'You see, he had the qualities I'd always been looking for, only they came in the most unexpected package.'

4 Read the text again. Mark the statements true (T) or false (F)?
1 Lady Sarah Moon felt happiness for the first time when she met her third husband, David. ☐
2 David shot himself accidentally while out shooting rabbits. ☐
3 When talking about David's death, Lady Sarah shows no emotion. ☐
4 Lady Sarah's second husband was unfaithful to her. ☐
5 She took revenge by destroying his expensive clothes, car and wine collection. ☐
6 Lady Sarah says that it was fear, rather than feminism, which drove her to behave the way she did. ☐
7 An expert in guns has suggested that David's death was not an accident. ☐
8 Lady Sarah doesn't believe that David would have had the courage to take his own life. ☐

5 Find words or phrases from the text to match the definitions.
1 rejected husbands/wives _____ (para 1)
2 rubber boots (UK – slang) _____ (para 3)
3 type of bird _____ (para 3)
4 quick _____ (para 4)
5 says loudly _____ (para 5)
6 type of armchair _____ (para 5)
7 fell to pieces _____ (para 7)
8 cut _____ (para 7)
9 completely destroyed (slang) _____ (para 7)
10 quick answer _____ (para 8)
11 have your revenge _____ (para 8)
12 dull and depressing _____ (para 11)

10.3

Reading

1 Read the story extract. Write sentences to connect the ideas from the story.

jumper/smoke

I took off my jumper so there wouldn't be a smell of smoke off it.

1 seagull/bread
2 builders/laughing
3 cement/names
4 building site/new road
5 night/watchmen
6 Christian names/doors
7 black marker/plastered wall
8 mother/hands

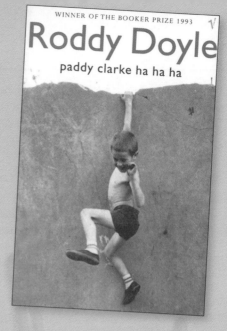

We lit fires. We were always lighting fires.

I took off my jumper so there wouldn't be a smell of smoke off it. It was cold now, but that didn't matter as much. I looked for somewhere clean to put the jumper. We were at the building site. The building site kept changing, the fenced-in part of it where they kept the diggers and the bricks and the shed the builders sat in and drank tea. There was always a pile of bread crusts outside the shed door, huge batch crusts with jam stains on the edges. We were looking through the wire fence at a seagull trying to pick up one of the crusts – it was too long for the seagull's beak – he should have grabbed it in the middle – when another crust came flying out the shed door and hit the side of the seagull's head. We heard the roars of the men's laughing from inside the shed.

  We'd go down to the building site and it wouldn't be there any more, just a square patch of muck and broken bricks and tyre marks. There was a new road where there'd been wet cement the last time we were there and the new site was at the end of the road. We went over to where we'd written our names with sticks in the cement, but they'd been smoothed over; they'd gone. 'Ah heck,' said Kevin.

  Our names were all around Barrytown, on the roads and paths. You had to do it at night when they were all gone home, except the watchmen. Then when they saw the names in the morning it was too late, the cement was hard. Only our Christian names, just in case the builders ever went from door to door up Barrytown Road looking for the boys who'd been writing their names in the wet cement.

  There wasn't only one building site; there were loads of them, all different types of houses.

  We wrote Liam's name and address with a black marker on a new plastered wall inside one of the houses. Nothing happened.

  My ma once smelt the smoke off me. She saw my hands first. She grabbed one of them. 'Look at your hands,' she said. 'Your fingernails!' Then she smelt me.

  'What have you been up to?'

  'Putting out a fire.'

  She killed me. The worst part was waiting to see if she'd tell me da when he got home.

da = dad

Grammar | uses of *would*

2 Add *would* or *wouldn't* to the sentences. Make any other necessary changes.

1 The boys light fires and play on building sites.
   _____

2 The builders find names written in cement in the morning.
   _____

3 The boys only write their Christian names so that the builders realise who they were.
   _____

4 The men throw their bread at the seagulls.
   _____

5 We have written all our names on the walls if we'd been brave enough.
   _____

6 She told me that we get into trouble if we went out at night.
   _____

7 You come over here and show me your hands, Patrick?
   _____

8 I wish she always tell my dad when I've been naughty.
   _____

3 Find the mistakes in the sentences and correct them.

1. He had always said that he will give me money.
2. The teacher wouldn't never smile at me.
3. Would you like follow me to my office?
4. The family moved to the countryside so that they would have had a better quality of life.
5. She warned us that the job would to be hard.
6. I'd have change jobs earlier if I had realise how easy it was.
7. No matter how hard they tried, the horse wouldn't to leave the stable.
8. Would you to turn the lights off when you have finished?

How to ... | describe a childhood memory

4 Complete the text using words from the box.

> however just sticks back always
> remember occasion felt hardly never

One memory that (1) _____ in my mind is of a mountain trip I did with my dad when I was young. My father was (2) _____ going off for the weekend climbing, and on this (3) _____ he said that I could go with him. I was only about seven years old, and he was planning a trip to Mount Sol-Ak in the eastern part of Korea. Mount Sol-Ak is one of the biggest mountains in Korea, and I had (4) _____ been on such a trip. I (5) _____ the feeling of excitement and anticipation the night before we left. We had to leave very early in the morning and I (6) _____ remember falling asleep on the train and waking to see the dawn at the bottom of the mountain. I can (7) _____ believe it now, but the first couple of hours' climbing were easy. (8) _____, as we climbed higher I could feel the sweat dripping down my body. I focussed on my father's words. 'If you can tolerate this pain now, you will be a better climber than me.' As my breathing became harder I (9) _____ tears swelling up in my eyes. But I had only one goal in mind: to reach the summit and become a better climber than my father. When we finally made it to the top my clothes were totally wet, but it didn't matter to me. I felt so proud and I thanked my father for his encouragement. I just remember feeling the fresh breeze, and watching the huge sun going down in the west. Looking (10) _____, I realise how the experience gave me confidence, and taught me a lesson in how to overcome problems.

Listening

5 **10.2** Cover the tapescript. Listen to the speaker describing a childhood memory. Answer the questions.

1. What experience does she describe?
2. Has she always enjoyed exams?
3. Why was she good at exams when she was younger?
4. What was different about the exams she took when she was at university?

6 Listen again. Complete the expressions in **bold**. Then match them to definitions a–g.

1. I think I might have been **a bit of a** _____ . ☐
2. I just wrote it out **word for** _____ . ☐
3. It was only _____ **in life**, when I came to do things like ... ☐
4. ... that you sort of **can't really** _____ **away with**. ☐
5. ... just **learning things by** _____ ☐
6. I got very _____ **out** for my A levels. ☐
7. I certainly _____ **the lesson** that ... ☐

a write down every word exactly as you learned/read it
b it is not sufficient
c nervous and tense
d someone who studies hard (often science) but doesn't fit in socially
e learned from experience
f a technique used by actors to memorise the lines of a play
g when I was older

TAPESCRIPT

I think I might have been a bit of a, a bit of a geek when I was very young, because I used to love exams, and, and not many people do that. But I think that's because I did a lot of acting, and so I used to learn, just learn very ... you know revise for exams as I did lines, and just learn it. So when it came to exam time, I just wrote it out word for word. And that's why I found my, my GCSEs particularly easy. It was only later in life, when I came to do things like A levels, and university exams that, where you have to apply theory, that you sort of can't really get away with just learning things by lines. I remember that I got very stressed out for my A levels, and I think I certainly learned the lesson that starting revision about three weeks before your exam is not a good idea. So, yeah, for me, childhood memories of exams were fun, and I always managed to do well, but later on in life it got a little bit more difficult.

Review and consolidation unit 10

Vocabulary

1 Write in the missing word in each sentence.
1. I'm in minds as to whether or not to go to the concert.
2. They are the moon about becoming grandparents.
3. He's been a bit in the dumps recently.
4. She was at her end about failing the exam.
5. Try not to get so wound about life. Take it easy.
6. I'm feeling particularly pleased myself for passing my driving test.
7. The kids have been out all day and they are with energy.
8. Now all the tickets are sold out so we're kicking.

Grammar | modals (and verbs with similar meanings)

2 Choose the correct words to complete the sentences.
1. They're _____ call us while they're over here.
   A need to   B bound to   C might to
2. We _____ get home because the babysitter is waiting.
   A 're bound to   B supposed to   C ought to
3. It _____ an easy decision to take.
   A can't have been   B couldn't to be
   C isn't bound to be
4. They _____ there earlier than we were expecting.
   A must have got   B mightn't have
   C would got
5. She _____ us if we had to bring something.
   A is supposed tell   B might tell
   C would have told
6. The house _____ need painting as nobody has lived there for ages.
   A would have   B can't   C is likely to
7. We _____ expected to do all the work by ourselves.
   A can't be   B ought to   C are likely to
8. She _____ asked before taking the car.
   A is bound to   B could have   C might
9. We _____ reply to the invitation before the 31st July.
   A need   B are supposed to   C would have
10. I _____ bring the spare copies after all.
    A 'm likely   B ought   C didn't need to

Vocabulary

3 One word in each sentence belongs in another sentence. Find the words and put them in the correct sentences.
1. At the beginning of the race, his chances of experiences seemed slim.
2. He has a tendency to want on the negative.
3. I'm sure it will all work out well in the long gut.
4. Try looking on the success side.
5. Generally, I would say I'm open to new run.
6. There are various techniques you can use to dwell your intuition.
7. I try to make sure I'm getting the things I really bright out of life.
8. My boost feeling is that things are going to be fine when we get there.

Vocabulary | strong adjectives of feeling

4 Choose the correct option.
1. We were *outraged/petrified/delighted* when she graduated from university with honours. We had always hoped that she would do well.
2. He was *furious/ecstatic/chuffed* when he realised his wallet had been stolen.
3. They were quite *terrified/taken aback/indifferent* when we told them the price. It was obviously a shock.
4. She was simply *thrilled/dumbstruck/uninterested* when she received the flowers. You could tell by her huge smile.
5. I'm a little *delighted/flabbergasted/indifferent* towards classical music. It doesn't do anything for me.
6. Most days she felt *miserable/taken aback/livid* and longed to see her friends and family at home.
7. I told him all about what had been happening, but he was completely *outraged/uninterested/ecstatic*. He just carried on watching the TV.
8. She was *terrified/livid/dumbstruck* that her parents would find out what she had been doing.
9. Katia was *livid/thrilled/ecstatic* when she saw the mess that the builders had left. She immediately rang the company to complain.
10. Eye witnesses were too *ecstatic/upset/taken aback* to talk about what had happened.

Grammar | uses of *would*

5 Add *would* or *wouldn't* to the text where appropriate.

When I was younger, my parents were always busy as they had just started their own business, so they often had to go abroad and couldn't look after my brother and me. When they went away on these trips, they send us to stay with my grandfather, a fruit farmer who lives at the foot of the mountains. I was always happy when my mother told us we stay with Grandpa, as the time we spent at his house was always wonderful. The air there is fresh and clean, and the scenery is beautiful. There is no pollution. In the morning I wake and smell the grass and the flowers, and hear the birds singing their song. There was an orchard filled with fruit trees of many kinds, and we were always happy when our grandfather asked: 'You like to help pick the fruit?' When the fruit was ripe, we could pick as much as we could eat. And when there was too much, we set up a street stall, and make good money selling the sweet fruit to passers-by.

My grandfather kept dogs and chickens, and took us for walks in the forest. Here he taught us the names of the plants, so that we know which were good to eat, which were useful for medicinal purposes, and which were toxic. He let us pick the plants until we could tell him what each one was. We learned so much when we were with him, more than we have learned by going to school. I have stayed there forever if it were possible.

Vocabulary | particles

6 Choose the correct alternative.

1 They have been *over/under/on* a lot of stress recently.
2 I've been handing *out/over/to* leaflets all morning.
3 Slow *up/down/off* – you're eating too fast!
4 Can you count *up/on/in* to 100 in Spanish?
5 Her husband ran *on/in/off* with a younger woman.
6 Will you lock *off/up/in* before you go to bed?
7 He's fifteen now, so he seems to spend most of his time just lounging *around/out/on*.
8 I can't believe that they just carried *off/on/at* smoking as if I wasn't even there!
9 I must write *in/on/down* the recipe for this dish. It's delicious.
10 I need some new jeans. My old ones have completely worn *in/out/on*.

Answer key

Unit 1 Challenges

Lesson 1.1
Reading
1 1 T 2 F 3 T 4 T 5 F 6 T 7 F 8 F 9 F
2a 1 set 2 face 3 rising 4 make 5 without 6 ambition 7 attitude 8 daunting
2b 1 Mount Everest was his lifetime ambition. However, first he climbed Mount Cook, the highest peak in New Zealand. Then he chose 26,906ft Mount Cho Oyu in Tibet, the world's sixth highest. And finally, he climbed Mount Everest. 2 He lost both his legs in an earlier climbing accident. He then broke one of his artificial legs on the way up, and had to replace it. He was also suffering with laryngitis. 3 Yes, he replaced the broken leg with a spare one, and continued to climb. 4 His 'childhood dream' was to 'stand on the roof of the world'. He managed to climb Mount Everest, despite his disability. 5 He couldn't have managed without a spare leg and parts. 6 She advises that they should never be limited in their ambitions. 7 Suggested answer: Mark seems to have the right attitude in that he persevered even when things got very tough. 8 Suggested answer: Climbing the highest mountain in the world, in sub-zero temperatures, without the use of your own legs is all very daunting. For me, perhaps the fact that he had to overcome his disability was the most daunting challenge.

Grammar: prepositions
3 1 for 2 from 3 in losing 4 from 5 to 6 about 7 on 8 from 9 of 10 with 11 in 12 about

Vocabulary: phrases about language
4 1 I've really let it slip. 2 I just picked up a few words when I was there on holiday. 3 A: How long did it take you to master the grammar? B: Years! I used to spend a lot of time cramming information from grammar books until I had complete information overload. 4 He left a garbled message which I can't understand. 5 The sheer delight of being able to talk to people I meet there. 6 Yes, she's very on the ball.

Listening
5 1 Polyglots have more 'white brain matter' in a part of the brain which processes sound. And their brains could also be less symmetrical than others. 2 It is hoped the research could be used help to identify reasons for language difficulties. 3 People were asked to distinguish between two similar sounds from different languages. 4 Good language learners were those who identified more than 80 percent of the sounds correctly, within a few minutes. 5 The fibres of the brain's white matter are involved with the efficient processing of sound by connecting the brain's regions together. 6 The brain scans could be used to diagnose clinical problems, or to predict whether someone has the ability to be good at something or not.

Lesson 1.2
Vocabulary: talking about how much you know
1 1 f 2 d 3 i 4 a 5 b 6 h 7 c 8 e 9 j 10 g

Reading and Grammar: passives
2 image is said to have haunted her
Martha is thought to have been   It is estimated that
Ishi is believed to be   He was thought to have left   it seems
3 1 winched 2 peering 3 haunted 4 fascination 5 flock 6 up to a mile 7 extinction 8 bulk 9 foothills 10 emerged
4 1 is said (that) 2 seems (that) 3 is claimed 4 is thought 5 is said 6 is/was thought 7 seems as 8 is thought 9 is believed 10 appears

Pronunciation: word stress
6 Suggested stress:
Foreign visitors to Naples are to be given cheap plastic watches as part of an attempt to combat the street crime for which the city has become notorious. Drug dealing, auto theft and street muggings are increasingly common crime trends creating problems for visitors and residents alike.
Moscow has been named the most expensive city in the world. Mercer, the human resources consultants, have compared costs internationally, of 200 items and concluded that the cost of living in the Russian capital is twelve percent higher than in London. Price rises in Moscow have been fuelled by a recent property boom.
More than eighty people were killed during gang violence in the state of Sao Paolo over the weekend in a wave of attacks on prisons and police stations. Most of the victims were police officers and prison guards, murdered in apparent retaliation for a criminal crackdown that began last month.
Hundreds of thousands of Spaniards have been demanding help from the government after losing their savings in a pyramid selling scam involving rare stamps. The 'Enron of Spain', as it has been labelled by experts, is the biggest financial scam that the country has ever known, and may have grave repercussions on the Spanish economy.

Lesson 1.3
Reading
1a 1 Extreme motorcycle races and rallies. 2 To be a true match for her male colleagues in these extreme races. 3 Her father helped her develop an interest in mechanics, and her mother gave her strong will power. 4 Broken bones, including her hand. 5 She 'shrieks' and carries on.
1b 1 crave 2 single-handedly 3 barely 4 quench her thirst for success 5 ultimate quest 6 be a true match 7 awed 8 desperate to 9 capable of 10 quit 11 will power 12 held on
1c 1 ultimate quest 2 single-handedly 3 quitting 4 barely 5 true match 6 craving 7 capable of

Vocabulary: achievement
2 1 begged 2 pursue 3 Constraints 4 faces 5 pushing 6 greatest triumphs 7 born 8 deal 9 persevered 10 heading

Grammar: perfect aspect
3 1 will have been 2 has travelled 3 has been (had been) 4 has/been requested 5 had/been 6 was 7 has had 8 gave up 9 set off 10 has been attacked 11 shot 12 has been 13 was rusting 14 have had

How to: talk about an achievement
4a 1 E 2 I 3 C 4 H 5 B 6 F 7 G 8 A 9 D

Review and consolidation unit 1

Passives
1 1 C 2 D 3 A 4 B 5 C 6 A 7 A 8 D 9 B 10 D
2 1 d 2 h 3 c 4 g 5 f 6 b 7 e 8 a

Perfect aspect
3 1 will have left/finished 2 realised we had 3 had been playing 4 hasn't been sleeping 5 won't have finished 6 I've left 7 had been trying 8 have been given/offered 9 hadn't heard 10 will have been working/will have worked
4 1 A 2 A 3 A 4 B 5 A 6 B

Prepositional phrases
5 1 appeal to 2 opt for 3 short of 4 nervous about 5 rely on 6 subject to 7 benefited from 8 reminiscent of 9 bother about 10 succeeded in

Vocabulary

6 **1** Paulo Freire? Who's he? I've never heard **of** him. **2** The Whorf-Sapir hypothesis? I know it like **in** the back of my hand. **3** Wendy's phone number? I don't know it **by** offhand. **4** Shakespeare's love poems? We spent years learning them by **the** heart. **5** Is Ronaldinho the best footballer in the world? Without **but** a doubt. **6** The Highway Code? Ask Susie – she's a driving instructor. She knows it inside **out**. **7** International banking? I know next **to** nothing about it. **8** Was Matisse the greatest painter in history? As far as I'm **concerned**, he was.

7a 1 unfit **2** overpaid **3** unmotivated **4** underestimate **5** non-smokers **6** non-/semi-professional **7** misunderstood **8** overworked **9** irrelevant **10** unaware

7b 1, 9, 11, 4, 3, 6, 5, 2, 7, 10, 8

Unit 2 Community

Lesson 2.1
Listening

1a Speaker 1 1 English **2** Colombia **3** Confused cansado and casado **4** wish I'd learned more of the language before moving
Speaker 2 5 Brazilian **6** U.S. **7** Cultural difference at gas station **8** felt a bit stupid
Speaker 3 9 Italian **10** England **11** Confused early and late **12** learn the basics

1c 1 ply **2** blunders **3** muddle through **4** perplexed **5** assigned **6** tearing my hair out

Grammar: verb patterns

2 1 to take **2** meeting **3** to write **4** of travelling **5** riding **6** to waste **7** you to reconsider **8** doing **9** to having to **10** us to go

3 1 of living **2** objecting **3** thinking **4** to change **5** afford to **6** find out **7** making **8** to take **9** advise you **10** to hearing

How to: give advice/make recommendations about places

4 1 d **2** j **3** h **4** e **5** f **6** b **7** i **8** a **9** c **10** g

Vocabulary: being polite

5a 1 you mind turning **2** I were you **3** Do you think **4** it be possible **5** were hoping you **6** wouldn't have thought

Lesson 2.2
Grammar: comparatives

1a Text 1 is more positive about Wikipedia than Text 2.

1b and 1c 1 It is **nowhere** near as complimentary about Wikipedia as the other text. Text 2 **2** It suggests that Wikipedia is **nothing** like as reliable as other encyclopaedias. Text 2 **3** It is **considerably more** positive about Wikipedia than the other text. Text 1 **4** The author of the text **would** rather let each generation question the views of the preceding generation. Text 1 **5** According to the text, the less we know about the contributors, **the** less we can trust Wikipedia. Text 2 **6** The author of the text is definitely not as critical of Wikipedia **as** the author of the other text. Text 1 **7** The author of the text probably thinks that rather **than** using Wikipedia for all research, you should only use it for simple facts. Text 2 **8** The text implies that it's **miles** better to let everyone contribute to encyclopaedias. Text 1

How to: recognise informal writing

2a 1 We look forward to hearing from you in due course. **2** Please don't hesitate to contact me if you have any queries. **3** Dear Mrs Dormer, **4** Technics Solutions would like to invite you to our annual investors meeting **5** inform us of your attendance by 14th June. **6** which will take place at The Atrium on Rose Street at 5.00p.m. on Wednesday 6th July. **7** We would be grateful if you could **8** Yours sincerely, Nicholas Spicer, Chairman, Technics Solutions

2b 3, 4, 6, 7, 5, 2, 1, 8

Reading

3a a 3 **b** 2 **c** 1

3b 1 eBay **2** boo.com **3** Amazon **4** eBay **5** boo.com **6** Amazon **7** eBay **8** boo.com

3c 1 bid **2** phenomenal **3** stock **4** reluctant **5** start-up **6** luxurious **7** doomed

Lesson 2.3
Listening

1a Speaker 1 says it's 'a hive of activity', e.g. music, football. They cheer and sing when Bafana Bafana plays.
Speaker 2 says the people are close to nature. The nature is wonderful, beautiful rainforests and coastlines. They grow their own food, so no one starves. People help each other. They are spiritual and not materialistic.
Speaker 3 says it's quiet. They are all old friends and have complementary skills.

1b 1 F **2** T **3** T **4** T **5** F **6** F **7** T **8** T **9** F
1c 1 A **2** B **3** C **4** C **5** C **6** C

Vocabulary: describing places

2 1 off the beaten track **2** heart **3** stunning **4** side by side **5** gaze **6** vast **7** stroll **8** run-down **9** diverse **10** packed **11** unspoilt **12** tranquil

Review and consolidation unit 2

Vocabulary

1 1 cost **2** infrastructure **3** mild **4** healthcare **5** standard **6** rate **7** Unemployment **8** pollution **9** tension **10** no-go **11** life **12** nightlife **13** cosmopolitan **14** freedom **15** monuments **16** congestion

Verb patterns

2 1 I'm thinking of **going** to France. What's the weather like in April? **2** Dave can't **afford** to take a holiday so he's camping in his garden this year! **3** Can you imagine **being** an astronaut? You could go into space! **4** Mario's so lazy: he always **avoids** doing the washing-up. **5** I tried to persuade Gail **to watch** a DVD tonight, but she didn't want to. **6** I can't **stand** smoking: cigarette smoke makes me ill. **7** They advised **us to use** traveller's cheques because they're safer. **8** I wouldn't **recommend** spending more than an hour or two in that museum. It's a bit dull. **9** My teachers always encouraged me **to do** my best. **10** Libby urged **us to enter** the competition. She was right: we won!

Comparatives

3 The online community is predicting that blogs will soon replace print journalism. While publishing news and views on the web is far easier **than** getting into print, I have my doubts about this prediction. Firstly, blogs are nowhere **near** as reliable as print journalism. There are checks and balances for print journalists, and newspapers are far **more** likely than websites to be prosecuted if they get the facts wrong. Reading a blog is much the same **as** reading a diary: if it is full of lies and exaggeration, there's not a lot you can do. The advantage of blogs is that they are personal and usually unedited. But **rather** than using them as formal carriers of news, I think we'd be better **off** having them as an alternative source of opinion. Basically, they act as a voice that cannot be silenced. The easier the web becomes to use, **the** more diverse voices it will contain, and that's a great thing. As for me, I **would** sooner read a newspaper any day!

4 1 S **2** D **3** S **4** D **5** S **6** D **7** D **8** S

Vocabulary

5 Across 1 value **2** wary **3** overrated **4** cracked
Down 3 out **5** overpriced **7** must **8** dull

6 1 charming **2** tranquil **3** off the beaten track **4** stroll **5** gaze **6** heart **7** side by side **8** packed **9** bustling **10** run down **11** unspoilt **12** vast

7 1 C **2** A **3** C **4** B **5** A **6** A **7** B **8** C

Unit 3 Tales

Lesson 3.1
Reading

1a 2

1b 1 What was *Every Day Over 100 is a Gift*? **2** Who was Miguel Carpiro? **3** What (according to the local people) happened to Carpiro's birth certificate? **4** Why might people in societies such as Abkhazian and Hunza lie about their age? **5** What did Mazess and Forman check (in Vilcabamba)? **6** Why did some World War 1 deserters use their dead parents' names?

1c 1 centenarians **2** causes a minor stir **3** plausible **4** revered **5** social status **6** brings about **7** deserters **8** detection

85

Grammar

2 1 At midnight, when we got back, she had already put the baby to bed.   2 The game was cancelled because it had been snowing.   3 Juan had been painting the bathroom.   4 I got home and discovered that my flat was being burgled.   5 Junichi told us he was training for the Olympics.   6 When I saw Joan she was going to the hairdressers.

3 1 were you talking   2 had been working   3 was barking
4 did you find   5 had met   6 hadn't been cleaned
7 Had you heard   8 had been talking   9 was being fixed
10 hadn't understood

Pronunciation

4 1 A   2 B   3 B   4 A   5 B   6 A   7 B   8 A

Lesson 3.2
Reading and Listening

1a 1 Thomas   2 A normal town, with a post office and High Street.   3 No, he spells 'birds' incorrectly.   4 Naughty (she stole her mother's make-up and she lies about the spelling of birds).   5 That it's funny and not true, but it shows the child's imagination.   6 Because she had stolen her mother's make-up and been caught.   7 He feels proud of them because they have good imaginations, even though they are naughty.   8 Suggested answer: surprising, surreal, funny

1b 1 poised   2 shriek   3 waddling   4 traipsing   5 fossilised
6 discarded   7 ruffled   8 glaring

1c 1 a large yellow-beaked eagle   2 a notebook   3 sound of seagulls   4 seagull   5 eyeshadow   6 penguin   7 father
8 swan

Vocabulary: describing books

2 1 turner   2 bestseller   3 base   4 account   5 depicts
6 hooked   7 bookworm   8 found   9 gripping
10 one-dimensional   11 down   12 avid

How to: describe people

3 1 across   2 get to know   3 strikes you   4 like about
5 such a   6 a bit

Vocabulary: compound adjectives

4a 1 single-minded   2 self-sufficient   3 thick-skinned
4 kind-hearted   5 stand-offish   6 career-orientated
7 level-headed   8 absent-minded

4b 1 single-minded and career-orientated   2 stand-offish
3 absent-minded   4 thick-skinned   5 kind-hearted

Lesson 3.3
Listening

1a A 1   B 3   C 2

1b 1 The driver was stopped because he was speeding.   2 There wasn't a gun in the glove box or a body in the boot.   3 A man wanted to get rid of a cat.   4 The man needed directions to get home.   5 The second note said 'blame everything on me'.
6 The manager's final problem was that the workers were on strike.

1c 1 SU   2 C   3 C   4 S   5 SU   6 C   7 SA

1d 1 1 and 5   2 1, 5 and 7. The emphasised words are *stole, gun, glove box* (1) and *gun, course* (5) and *bet, liar, speeding* (7)
3 2, 3, 4 and 6

Grammar

2 1 ✓   2 On **being** arrested by the police, Teresa admitted that she was guilty of fraud.   3 She broke her leg while **playing** hockey.   4 ✓   5 **Helping** other people wasn't something that usually made Mrs Davies happy.   6 ✓   7 All of the boys, **hoping** to be football stars, trained for six hours every day.   8 ✓   9 Having **woken** up at 4.00 a.m., we were exhausted by 11.00.   10 After **listening** to the speech for four hours, Bianca eventually fell asleep.

3 1 cheating   2 Having been caught   3 playing   4 Called
5 asking   6 celebrating   7 Betting   8 Having made   9 involved
10 telling   11 having placed   12 known

Vocabulary

4
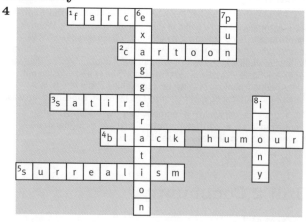

Review and consolidation unit 3

Vocabulary

1 1 B   2 C   3 B   4 C   5 A   6 C   7 C   8 A

Narrative tenses review

2 1 had been driving   2 was being turned into   3 had left
4 had been memorising   5 was making   6 had been writing
7 hadn't read   8 was facing   9 had been borrowed   10 Did/get up

Vocabulary

3
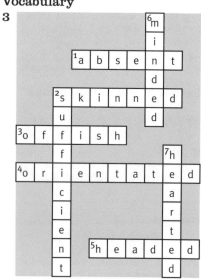

4 1 Yolanda seems **to** be a very nice girl.   2 You're such a fast swimmer I could never keep up with you.   3 **The** thing I don't like about Samantha is that she's so selfish.   4 The thing **that** strikes you about Gudrun is her determination.   5 He can be a bit annoying sometimes but his heart's in the right place.   6 Once you get to know Maurice, you'll like him.

5 1 satire   2 farce   3 puns   4 cartoons   5 surreal humour
6 black humour

Participle clauses/gerunds

6 1 Hoping   2 Restored/Having been restored
3 Running   4 sat/sitting   5 While driving   6 On hearing/Having heard   7 Buried   8 After being caught/Having been caught   9 taken/being taken   10 After being treated/Treated

Vocabulary

7 1 It is a dead-end job.   2 Maggie and Denis have a stormy relationship.   3 That was the moment when her career took off.   4 It's the manager who's in the firing line.   5 They gave me a frosty reception.   6 I'd never wanted to follow in my mother's footsteps.   7 Once you get promoted, you'll have to call the shots.   8 He has his sights set on becoming a fighter pilot.
9 We'd reached a crossroads.   10 Several of us were feeling a bit under the weather.

Unit 4 Progress

Lesson 4.1
Vocabulary: progress
1a 1 f 2 c 3 h 4 e 5 d 6 a 7 g 8 b
b 1 software company 2 genetic engineering 3 shuttle launch 4 skin tissue 5 orbit / moon 6 test tube 7 rare strain 8 computer network

Reading
2 Making a superhero – fact or fiction?

Grammar: future probability/possibility/certainty
3 1 The odds are against being born on another planet. 2 I doubt whether you would find a cosmic lantern. 3 Gamma rays are definitely produced by nuclear explosions. 4 There's every likelihood that if Dr Banner had received this radiation, he would have died. 5 There's a slim chance we could create a believable version of hulk in reality. 6 Giving him anabolic steroids would almost definitely/certainly create his pumped-up look. 7 These might well cause him to become more aggressive and moody. 8 There is a remote possibility that we could create green skin by genetic engineering. 9 A radioactive spider could conceivably exist. 10 An animal stands no chance of transferring DNA via a bite. 11 If it did transfer its DNA, it wouldn't stand a chance of fusing with our DNA. 12 If ingesting DNA was enough to change our own DNA, we would presumably adopt the characteristics of chickens and apples when we ate them. 13 Batman might well be the most realistic of the heroes. 14 There is a distinct possibility that modern carmakers could even create a batmobile.

4 1 any/slim 2 against/possibility 3 no 4 doubt 5 well 6 bound 7 doubtful 8 conceivably 9 likelihood 10 chances

Listening
5a 1 Because she was able to lift the heavy car off the boy like the superhero Wonder Woman. 2 To comfort a mother and child trapped in the house by a fire.
5b 1 1.7 metres tall 2 one-tonne car 3 trapped underneath 4 severely injured 5 good recovery 6 found the strength 7 thinking of her own son 8 an award 9 outstanding bravery 10 rescue a mother and child 11 daring climb 12 front of the building 13 in the smoke-filled room 14 the fire-fighters arrived

Lesson 4.2
Vocabulary: talking about plans/free time
1 1 B 2 A 3 C 4 C 5 A 6 C 7 C 8 A 9 B 10 C

Grammar: future tenses review
2 1 're going to 2 I'll 3 I'm leaving 4 will be doing 5 will have gone 6 you decide 7 would 8 'll 9 'll have finished 10 leaves

Reading
3 1 F 2 F 3 T 4 T 5 F 6 F 7 T 8 T 9 T 10 F
4a 1 anxious (to do something) 2 embarked 3 savouring 4 godfather 5 backlash 6 folly 7 gauge 8 itch
4b 1 embarked 2 anxious 3 savour 4 gauge 5 backlash

How to: sound vague
5a 1 less 2 time 3 moon 4 bits 5 ish 6 about 7 of 8 of

Lesson 4.3
Vocabulary
1 1 demanding 2 gifted 3 making 4 prodigy 5 adulation 6 peers 7 freaks

Reading
2 Obsessed with cameras as a toddler
Starred in Goddess of the Village – aged four
Role in Papa Pandu – soap opera
Wrote a hit song for a film – aged six
Appeared in twenty-four films and more than 1000 episodes of the soap opera.
Wrote a short story about Bangalore street kids
Later turned the story into a screenplay C/o Footpath
Director of his own film – aged nine. Youngest director in the world.

3 1 He has always been involved in film. He enjoys playing, but not as much as other children. He doesn't go to school very often. 2 He was 'obsessed with the camera' even as a toddler. His behaviour would improve when his parents were filming him. He won an audition for his first film part aged four. 3 He was always asking staff on the set of the soap about the various shots. When he wrote his own short story, he turned it into a screenplay, and then decided to direct the film himself. 4 He met some street children who were selling newspapers on a busy road. Talking to them he discovered that they were orphans who would be beaten if they didn't return home with money. He was moved by the encounter. 5 He would like the children to watch it and want to go to school. He also wants to be the youngest director in the world. 6 His secretary collects notes for him when he misses lessons. 7 His father worries that his son is missing out on his childhood, because he doesn't play like other children.

4a 1 barking orders 2 affluent 3 urged 4 (be) obsessed with 5 beaten 6 be moved by 7 encounter 8 prop 9 keep up 10 reassure

4b director edit suite cuts a shot leading film star scene making movies be in films/appear in episodes of a soap opera the director's seat (film) be successful fans favourite actors Bollywood superstar acting career an audition given a part fantasy adventure land a lead role daily (Bangalore) soap wrote a hit song obsessed with cameras camera 'was on him' this shot/that shot journalists screenplay during filming frame give the shot depth

Grammar: inversion
5 1 had we heard 2 Not only did she 3 everyone has arrived 4 have I been 5 Not since I went 6 am I going 7 Only if 8 do you need to 9 did I 10 is the service great

6 1 Nowhere 2 Only 3 until 4 sooner 5 Not 6 Nowhere 7 before 8 Only 9 Only 10 Never

Review and Consolidation unit 4

Vocabulary
1 1 A 2 B 3 C 4 B 5 A

Future probability
2 1 The odds are against them winning the series. 2 We're bound to see her on the flight. 3 The chances are that it will rain later. 4 It is doubtful that we will have time to finish everything today. 5 There is a distinct possibility that we'll beat the competition. 6 There is every likelihood that he'll get the promotion. 7 That may well prove to be an excellent idea. 8 There is a slim chance that we could catch the earlier train.

Vocabulary
3

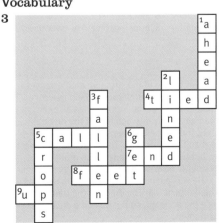

87

Future tenses review
4 1 'll call 2 will/'ll have finished 3 is coming
4 'm going to do/'ll do/'m doing 5 is going to be 6 'll take
7 'm meeting 8 'm going to be 9 'll see 10 'll get/'m going to get

How to: sound vague
5 1 time 2 once 3 bits 4 less 5 way 6 sort 7 kind 8 so

Inversion
6 1 Not only **did** they apologise for the inconvenience, but they have refunded the money! 2 ✓ 3 Only **after** I repeatedly asked them, did I manage to get a response. 4 Not since 2005 **has there** been such a hot summer. 5 ✓ 6 Never before **have we** been able to photograph these small creatures in such detail. 7 Only if we keep looking **will we** ever find the solution. 8 ✓ 9 Not for one minute did **I think** they really meant what they said. 10 Nowhere **does it** say that we aren't allowed to use this room.

Vocabulary
7 1 order 2 By 3 trial 4 regulations 5 aches 6 tried
7 facts 8 about 9 once 10 ready 11 again 12 tired
13 pieces 14 time 15 less

Unit 5 Fortunes

Lesson 5.1
Vocabulary
1 1 fortune 2 haggle 3 stock 4 rise 5 high-income
6 priceless 7 commission 8 bankrupt
2 1 cool 2 fraud 3 span 4 experience 5 funds 6 bouquet
7 profit 8 hope

Grammar: emphasis
3 1 The fact that 1 in 10 children in the UK are suffering from a mental health disorder is very worrying indeed. 2 Americans are not very interested in soccer at all. They prefer to watch baseball. 3 It is by no means certain that giving aid is the best way to help poorer countries. 4 Kandinsky even abandoned his law studies in order to train as an artist in Munich. Or Even Kandinsky abandoned his law studies in order to train as an artist in Munich. 5 The reason why the most popular soap opera in South American history, I Am Betty The Ugly, was so successful is because the woman who played Betty was incredibly beautiful. 6 The person who planted the UK's first ever olive grove in 2006 was Marco Diacono. He hoped that global warming would help the trees to survive. 7 We went to the Pantanal, in Brazil, to enjoy the wildlife, but I did get a shock when I found an 8ft-long caiman (alligator) outside my tent. 8 The place I would suggest you stay is along the coast from Amalfi.

4 1 c 2 g 3 e 4 a 5 b 6 d 7 h 8 f

Reading and Listening
5 1 She remembers him being at home when she did her first tap debut, aged four and her parents having an argument. 2 Because they were frightening to a small child in this difficult situation. 3 She had her fingerprints taken, searched, and had her bag searched. 4 The girl was quiet and serious, nervous (hot), and sad. 5 She could touch him through the fence with her fingers, or with a kiss. 6 The way her father dressed, how he walked, talked and smiled.

6 1 tap dancing debut 2 a heated argument 3 a teepee
4 moccasins 5 humm, clang 6 inmates
7 giant stainless-steel counter 8 buzz 9 hive 10 sauntered

Lesson 5.2
Vocabulary
1 1 The manager took advantage **of** the situation and increased his own salary. 2 The army have volunteered **to** help move people out of the disaster area. 3 The furniture has all been reduced so now you can get nearly fifty percent **off** the original price. 4 Unfortunately, the footballer gave his wife **power** of attorney, and she spent all the money. 5 The local farmers invested in the water company, but never saw a **penny** of the profit that was made. 6 The residents have been pestering the government **to** change the law. 7 He was a media millionaire, but after the scandal he **declared** bankruptcy. 8 The driver of the train hasn't been able to work since the accident, so he lives off a disability **pension** from the government.

Grammar: conditionals
2 1 If I had my car here, I would offer you a lift. 2 I'll make some coffee if everyone has finished eating. 3 If it hadn't been for Jamie, we would have waited for ages. 4 If you had listened carefully to what I said, this wouldn't have happened! 5 Provided that she has all the right injections, she will (or should) be fine. 6 If only they had rung us ten minutes earlier, we would have cancelled the order. 7 Unless Graham changes his strategy, the business will (or could) go bankrupt. 8 Should you happen to be in Oxford, you should (or must) come and stay. 9 Supposing they offered her the job, would she accept it? 10 I don't mind how much it costs, so long as the job is finished by Sunday.

3 1 Provided that the team keep playing as they are at the moment, we have a good chance of winning the cup. 2 Should you happen to see Martin on your travels, could you tell him I've been trying to contact him? 3 If it hadn't been for Kate telling us, we never would have realised what they were planning. 4 If you would like to see they rest of the house, I can leave you a key and you can show yourself around. 5 If only we hadn't bought the tickets already, then we could change our plans. 6 As long as Sheila still works there, she should be able to give you all the information you need.

Vocabulary: charity
4 1 fortune 2 donating 3 Foundation 4 mission 5 charity
6 generosity 7 impact 8 dedicate 9 deal 10 inspired
11 lavishly 12 admirable 13 vision

Reading
5 1 There are sixty-four new millionaires reportedly created everyday in Silicone Valley. 2 Many of the people who find themselves suddenly rich are in their twenties and thirties.
3 He noticed a change about ten years ago, when people from middle-class backgrounds started coming into money.
4 The number of millionaires in the United States and Canada at the time of the article. 5 The number of hours a week that people would work on their new business until they became rich. 6 The age at which many of these millionaires can retire. 7 The amount of money Rory Holland made when he sold his company in 1998.

6 1 The rise in internet-based businesses. 2 They may feel guilt, stress and confusion. These feelings may make them experience panic attacks, feel depressed, suffer insomnia etc. 3 The 'new' rich, who grew up without wealth, and expected to spend their lives working are likely to suffer. 4 Anxiety and depression may be caused by watching the stock market. 5 He suggests becoming involved in the community through fundraising projects etc.
7 He feels that they should be treated with sympathy.

7 1 handle 2 crave 3 drawbacks 4 rip apart
5 fledgling 6 mid-life crisis 7 entitled 8 upbringing

Lesson 5.3
Vocabulary
1

		¹e											
		n			²d								
³c	⁴o	n	v	e	n	i	e	n	c	e			
	p				v								
⁵p	e	r	k	s			⁶s	u	⁷p	p	o	r	t	i	v	e
o	n				l				r				
r	n				o	⁸a			o				
t	m				p	c		⁹s	a	l	¹⁰a	r	y
u	e				m	h			p			u	
n				¹¹f	l	e	x	i	b	l	e		
i	t			n	e	c			t			o	
t				t	v	t			s			n	
i				e								o	
¹²p	e	n	s	i	o	n			m			m	
s								¹³c	h	a	l	l	e	n	g	i	n	g
								t					
							¹⁴s	a	t	i	s	f	a	c	t	i	o	n

How to: express priorities

2a and c **1** The <u>essential</u> thing for <u>me</u> is to be <u>able</u> to walk to <u>work</u>. **2** <u>Having</u> good <u>promotion</u> prospects is <u>absolutely vital</u>. **3** <u>Having</u> flexible <u>working</u> hours <u>isn't</u> a major <u>priority</u>. **4** My <u>main priority</u> is <u>job</u> satisfaction. **5** I <u>couldn't do</u> without <u>supportive colleagues</u>. **6** I'm <u>not</u> really <u>bothered</u> about <u>having a pension plan</u>.

Grammar: sentence adverbials

3 **1** Believe it or not, sales figures were up on last year. **2** Apparently, the company is losing a lot of money. **Or** The company is apparently losing a lot of money. **3** Broadly speaking, the management have a good relationship with the rest of the staff. **4** In my opinion, the conclusions of the report are fundamentally wrong. **5** I'd like to say no to the extra work, but on the other hand, I need the money. **6** What you say is true, but only up to a point. **7** I travel a lot for my job. By and large I enjoy it although it can be exhausting. **8** With hindsight, we should probably have approached them earlier. **9** Surprisingly enough, the results of the survey indicate that there could be a good market for the new product.

Listening

4a **1** She is a business expert. **2** It is an innovative media company.

4b **Creative ideas and strange food:** To encourage their staff to be more creative they offer chocolate ants to their workers, and serve crocodile curry for lunch.
Inspiring the workers: There is a Director of Freshness who comes up with new ideas like working in the park on a sunny day, or having magicians in the office.
Number of employees/average age of workers: 389 employees, most under thirty-five years old
Schemes and new ideas: There was a scheme called 'If I ran the company' where workers could give their ideas. They introduced a bar which serves free breakfasts and stays open at night.

Vocabulary: expressing quantity

5 **1** plenty **2** not **3** awful **4** little **5** vast **6** deal **7** most **8** many **9** few

Review and consolidation unit 5

Vocabulary

1 **1** i **2** e **3** j **4** b **5** a **6** h **7** d **8** c **9** f **10** g

Conditional sentences

2 **1** If it hadn't been for the weather, we would have had a wonderful holiday. **2** You can use my phone provided that you don't speak for too long. **3** If only I had listened to her advice! **4** Should you happen to be in Rome, you should call my sister. **5** Supposing we were to call the police, that might help. **6** If you would let us know as soon as the parcel arrives. **7** As long as he lives in that house, I'm not going back there.

Emphasis

3 **1** B **2** C **3** A **4** A **5** B **6** B **7** C **8** C

4 Crossword:
- 4 across: mission
- 6 across: fortune
- 11 across: lavishly
- 12 across: greedy
- 1 down: g...
- 2 down: v...
- 3 down: i...
- 5 down: p...
- 7 down: i... m
- 8 down: p
- 9 down: c...
- 10 down: d

5 **1** satisfaction **2** supportive **3** promotion **4** challenging **5** development **6** recognition **7** flexible **8** convenience

6 **1** by and large ~~however~~ broadly speaking **2** ~~Essentially~~ On the other hand However **3** believe it or not surprisingly enough ~~with hindsight~~ **4** With hindsight Looking back ~~However~~ **5** essentially ~~looking back~~ fundamentally **6** ~~on the other hand~~ apparently seemingly

Idioms: money

7 **1** He sold his business for $14 million. He's **worth** a fortune. **2** As a student I lived **on/off** the money I earned from waitressing jobs. **3** Since my husband lost his job, we're not very well **off** financially. **4** I have spent this month's salary, so now I **am** completely broke. **5** You don't need to pay for everything. Let's split the bill. **6** You should treat **yourself** to something special at least once a month. **7** It's a beautiful dress, and the best thing about it is that it was dirt **cheap**. **8** Let's splash **out** on a meal in an expensive restaurant. **9** I shouldn't worry about paying back the money. She's rolling **in** it. **10** My wage brings us more than enough to get **by** on. **11** I'm glad you like the carpet. It cost me an **arm** and a leg. **12** It's very expensive to buy on my own, but perhaps we could **go halves**.

Unit 6 Power

Lesson 6.1
Listening

1a **1** To make a list of the new seven wonders of the world. **2** They are all on the shortlist. **3** They have been destroyed over the years by a combination of earthquakes, fire, and greed.

1b **The voting process:** done by the public on the Internet
Bernard Weber: he launched the campaign. He is an adventurer, film-maker and entrepreneur
Criticisms of the new list: a professor at Johns Hopkins University says the Internet should be on the list because it allows us to access all the other wonders

1c **1** B **2** A **3** B **4** A **5** A **6** B **7** B

Grammar: articles

3 **1** a **2** the **3** – **4** the **5** – **6** an **7** – **8** the **9** the **10** –

How to: describe an important building/structure

4 **1** The Taj Mahal is probably **the** most famous building in India. **2** The Ice Hotel, Quebec, is entirely **made from** ice. **3** Maya Ying Lin designed a famous wall in Washington DC **as a** memorial for the soldiers who died in Vietnam. **4** The Arc de Triomphe, Paris, was built **in honour** of Napoleon's military conquests. **5** ✓ **6** The Great Wall of China is around 4000 miles long and 7.5 **metres high**. **7** The Mayan pyramids may have been used **to house** the bodies of kings. **8** Turkey's greatest church, the Hagia Sophia, is said to have **been** built in just five years.

Lesson 6.2
Reading

1a 2

1b **1** accessible/approachable **2** email **3** many **4** inappropriate **5** tone **6** presume/expect **7** time **8** class(es) **9** certain/sure **10** rules

1c 2, 3, 5 and 7 are true

1d **1** skipped **2** petulant **3** legitimacy **4** draft **5** deference **6** invaluable **7** a blind spot **8** hit on the best solution

Grammar: whatever/whoever/whenever/however

2 **1** No matter who you are, you have to pay $10 to get in. **2** Giles is your driver. Wherever you want to go, he will take you. **3** ✓ **4** However you look at it, whether you are staff or customers, it's a stupid rule. **5** ✓ **6** Whatever you said, I didn't hear you because of the music. **7** ✓ **8** Whoever you spoke to, it wasn't the boss, but a criminal impersonator! **9** ✓ **10** My mum told me I had that mark when I was born. **11** ✓ **12** However you choose to join, whether online or in person, it is a great deal.

3 **1** why **2** whenever **3** Whatever **4** when **5** Whoever **6** Wherever

Vocabulary: phrasal verbs

4 **1** How do you manage to keep coming up with so many great ideas? **2** The concert will kick off with a half-hour set by the grunge band, Easy Daze. **3** This is our new product. We're hoping it will catch on in the Far East especially. **4** Revolutions tend to come about because of desperation on a huge scale. **5** According to fashion guru Leila Wintour, lacy stockings are in this winter, and every woman should have a pair. **6** It can be difficult to keep up with the news on the island because the post only comes once a month and there's no Internet. **7** The company decided to home in on new technology, focussing its attention on digital software. **8** While hats were fashionable last summer, they seem to be out this year.

Lesson 6.3
Listening

1a **1** T **2** T **3** F **4** F **5** T

1b **1** whatsoever **2** self-obsessed **3** stream of nonsense **4** for/loudmouth **5** cynical **6** eye-opener

Grammar

2 **1** despite **2** On arriving **3** When **4** despite **5** in spite **6** She hardly falls asleep **7** as long as the festival is **8** Although

3 **1** C **2** B **3** A **4** C **5** A **6** C **7** B **8** C **9** B **10** A

Vocabulary: describing people

4

			¹c	h	a	r	i	s	m	a	t	i	c	
		²d	i	g	n	i	f	i	e	d				
³i	d	e	a	l	i	s	t	i	c					
			⁴a	p	p	r	o	a	c	h	a	b	l	e
				⁵t	i	r	e	l	e	s	s			
				⁶t	r	u	s	t	w	o	r	t	h	y
			⁷w	a	v	e	r							
⁸c	o	r	r	u	p	t								
		⁹d	r	i	v	e								
			¹⁰n	o	n	d	e	s	c	r	i	p	t	
	¹¹d	o	w	n	-	t	o	-	e	a	r	t	h	
			¹²g	r	a	v	i	t	a	s				
	¹³r	e	s	o	l	u	t	e						

Key word: inspirational

Review and consolidation unit 6
Articles

1 **1** **Dogs** are generally considered the best pets for the elderly. **2** We thought we heard **a** burglar, but later we realised that the noise was actually the pipes. **3** He **climbed Mount** Kilimanjaro when he was still a teenager. **4** As a child, she learned to play **the** piano, and later went on to become a composer. **5** I'll see you in **the** supermarket at 8.00. Don't be late! **6** It's hard for people like me to diet, because **I love chocolate**. **7** The UK has introduced **a** law to help newly-arrived immigrants to find work. **8** I crossed **the** Pacific Ocean in an old wooden boat! **9** **The** Italian national anthem is one of my favourites. **10** We spoke to **the** Chief Executive of the company last night.

whatever/whoever/whenever

2 **1** B **2** A **3** A and B **4** A and B **5** A **6** A and B

Link words of time and contrast

3 **1** hardly **2** at which point **3** Much **4** when **5** had no sooner **6** On **7** While **8** In spite

4 **1** g **2** h **3** e **4** c **5** f **6** a **7** d **8** b

Phrasal verbs

5 **1** You must keep up with developments in your field. **2** Those trousers are in at the moment. **3** The idea came about because of something I read. **4** The company is homing in on the children's market. **5** It's hard to keep coming up with new ideas all the time. **6** That fashion will catch on very quickly. **7** His appearance on MTV in those shoes kicked off a major new trend. **8** Style gurus tell us that long hair is out.

Vocabulary

6 **1** B **2** C **3** C **4** A **5** C **6** B **7** C **8** B

7 **1** solar **2** brain **3** world **4** consumer **5** in positions **6** comes to **7** special powers

8 **1** We are setting these rules because we have **your interests** at heart. **2** Sorry, but you need to **face the music**. You just aren't good enough. **3** Cheryl's found a great new job. She always seems to **land on her feet**. **4** I'm **an old hand** at these things so I'll show you what to do. **5** On friday the problem finally **came to a head**. **6** Can you help me with this photocopying? I'm absolutely **rushed off** my feet. **7** We solved the problem and managed to **save face**. **8** When I saw my disastrous exam result, my **heart sank**. **9** That company went bankrupt because the boss didn't have a good **head for business**. **10** Sorry, she can't help you. She has **her hands full**.

Unit 7 Nature

Lesson 7.1
Reading

1a **1** B **2** C **3** C **4** B

1b **1** remunerated **2** traces **3** scrubbed **4** minute **5** hone **6** no hard feelings

1c chief constable   training regime   crime scene   sense of smell dog handlers   film star   washing powder   in demand

1d **1** film star **2** in demand **3** sense of smell **4** washing powder **5** crime scene **6** dog handlers **7** training regime **8** chief constable

Grammar: relative clauses

2 **1** A **2** C **3** B **4** B **5** A **6** B **7** C **8** A

3 **1** It was Juan who ate all the chocolate. That's why he's feeling sick! **2** When I was lost, I asked four people, none of who knew the way. **3** These are the books (that/which) I paid for. These two were free. **4** Last week, we fixed these computers, all of which work OK now. **5** This form must be completed before the conference. Please tick the topic in which you are interested. **6** I spoke to the woman whose brother works with my wife.

Vocabulary: collocations

4 **1** By watching the movements of animals, we can predict natural **disasters** such as earthquakes and tidal waves. **2** There are many stories of drowning people being carried to **safety** by dolphins; these may be true because dolphins rescue animals the same size as themselves. **3** Animal **instincts** often allow animals to escape from danger that humans don't notice. **4** Rescue teams work with dogs because of the dogs' excellent **sense** of smell. **5** Birds used to save **lives** during wartime by carrying vital messages to army commanders. **6** In the dark, cats and bats see things that are **invisible** to the human eye.

How to: explain procedures

5 Olaf Sund says that teaching a parrot to talk is a piece **of** cake. Here he gives a few invaluable tips.

The first thing you've **got** to do is choose the right bird. Bigger birds, like Blue Fronts and Yellow Napes, are your best bet, and make sure you get them when they are young. Birds older than eighteen months probably won't learn to talk.

Once you've chosen the bird, put it in the room where the family congregates the most – maybe the living room. For parrots to learn how to talk, human interaction is the key.

At first it can be a bit **tricky** for any wild animal in a domestic environment, so give the bird a few weeks to acclimatise. The next **step** is to turn off the TV and remove any distractions. Place the bird on your hand, and say a word in conjunction with an action or object. For example, give it a peanut and say: 'Peanut' or lift the bird up and say: 'Up'. The process must be pretty **straightforward**, so use short simple words at first.

Be gentle and patient with the bird and **put** lots of emotion in your voice. Teach the bird in fifteen-minute sessions, and give rewards such as food when the bird repeats a word. Without doing **this**, some birds are slow to speak. **If** your teaching doesn't work, you should allow another family member to try. Many birds prefer a female voice.

Lesson 7.2
Reading and Listening
1a 1 Where has he seen/did he see acres of cracked earth? **2** Why do you/does he follow the trails of animals? **3** Why should you look at the rocks? **4** What does the waterfall sound like? **5** Where have the birds made their home? **6** Whose boat crashed into the reef? **7** How old is the Great Barrier Reef? **8** Why does he call the Great Barrier Reef the biggest living organism in the world?

1b 1 To show how hot the weather was in Arizona. **2** Because the sun burns your skin and you peel. **3** 'The roaring, like some great giant's endless breath' and 'endless tongues of screaming white water' **4** Because they live in the middle of the waterfall, which is very loud. **5** There are many beautiful precious things there and it is very colourful.

1c 1 acre **2** blazing **3** grovel **4** chasm **5** spray **6** jammed **7** cataract **8** rammed **9** beams **10** translucent

Grammar
2 1 1 B 2 A **2** 1 A 2 B **3** 1 B 2 A **4** 1 B 2 A **5** 1 B 2 A **6** 1 A 2 B

3 1 taking **2** to experience **3** travelling **4** to become **5** to go **6** to stay **7** leaving **8** making

Vocabulary
4 1 b **2** f **3** h **4** i **5** a **6** j **7** e **8** g **9** d **10** c

Lesson 7.3
Grammar: *as ... as* and describing quantity
1 1 g **2** c **3** b **4** e **5** h **6** d **7** f **8** a

2 1 This one's **a great deal** cheaper than that one. **2** I'm told that **virtually** all of them passed – only two people had to retake the exam. **3** Our courses cost **as little as** $224.99 per week, an absolute bargain! **4** Your suitcase weighs exactly fifty kilos, which is **well over** the limit! **5** This lift takes **a maximum of** ten people. **6** A **tiny minority of** people wanted Jones to win, but everyone else voted for Smith. **7** During the winter, sometimes we get **as few as** six or seven tourist groups a week. **8** I need **precisely** one hundred and twenty three of those bottles. No more, no less!

Vocabulary
4a 1 'Well, yes, it's used, but it's in great condition. This really is a rare opportunity because it's **the** latest model, as I'm sure you realise. Everything's in working order, though I haven't tried the brakes yet. And don't worry about that **wear and tear** on the tyres. They'll be fine.' **2** 'This one is a very rare opal stone. It really is one **of** a kind. Over a thousand years ago it was worn by a tribal queen. Despite its age, you can see that it is in perfect **condition**.' **3** 'These are all made **by** hand. We pick the fruit in the morning, chop it up and coat it in sugar and honey. Then we roll the pastry and put the fruit inside it. You can choose from a **selection** of over fifteen fruits.' **4** 'This model has only been on the **market** for a few weeks and it's unbelievable: you've got wide-screen vision, anti-reflection technology, and it even features an intelligent remote control that knows your viewing tastes. It's absolutely **state-of-the-art** and it's yours, brand new, for just $10,000.' **5** 'OK, OK, they're second-hand but they're as **good** as new. I mean, look, they're still in their packaging! They come in a wide **range** of colours and sizes, and the lenses are just fantastic. What do you mean, 'the sun's not going to come out'?'

Listening
6b Speaker 1: Scientist (who uses animals in experiments); Yes. For using animals in experiments; Yes. Says 'the experiments are for the benefit of humankind. Without them, modern medicine would be in medieval times.'; The interviewer is against animal testing: 'isn't it the mice, the monkeys, the animals, that are suffering?' and gives statistics that we can't 'justify'.
Speaker 2: Works for the RSPCA, a charity that protects animals; No; No; The interviewer is amazed at the problem: 'It seems impossible in this day and age that these things can still happen.'
Speaker 3: circus manager; Yes. For having animals in the circus: 'It was pressure from outside.'; He says the animals were treated extremely well.; The interviewer is against using animals in the circus: 'we know they were taken from their natural environment and basically captured and trained to entertain people.'

Review and consolidation unit 7
Vocabulary
1 animal, breed, carnivore, dog, endangered, fur, guide, hibernate, instincts, koala, lay, mammal, natural, over-fishing, predator, reserve, sanctuary, tame, vaccination, web

Relative clauses
2 1 A **2** B **3** B **4** A and B **5** A **6** B **7** A and B **8** A and B **9** B **10** A

Verb patterns
3 1 I decided to stop **smoking** because my lungs were in bad shape. **2** That sweet little boy went on **to become** the President. **3** They regretted **paying** so much money for such a terrible meal. **4** Will you remember **to feed** the cat while I'm away? **5** I tried **to warn** you about that horrible man but you wouldn't listen. **6** During the trip we stopped **to buy** petrol a couple of times. **7** We asked her to be quiet but she just went on **talking** throughout the film. **8** It was an accident – I didn't mean **to spill** that water all over her computer! **9** Do you remember **playing** that game when we were children? **10** She tried **drinking** hot milk before bed, but nothing would work – she still couldn't sleep. **11** This new job means **leaving** our hometown to go and live abroad. **12** I regret **to inform** you that your contract has been terminated with immediate effect.

Vocabulary
4 1 C **2** A **3** C **4** B **5** C **6** A **7** C **8** A **9** B **10** C

as ... as and describing quantity
5 1 majority **2** Virtually **3** minority **4** few **5** approximately **6** way under **7** great deal **8** minimum

Vocabulary
6a 1 j **2** h **3** i **4** c **5** f **6** b **7** e **8** g **9** a **10** d
6b 1 It comes in a wide range **2** It's made by hand **3** It's brand new **4** It's one of a kind **5** It's on the market
7a and b 1 Breaking up a dog fight can be very tricky. 1 **2** If you hit the dog, it will attack you! 3 **3** The next thing you've got to do is to walk the dog backwards. 4 **4** Finally, tie the dogs away from each other. 7 **5** Secondly, get help. 4 **6** Firstly, don't hit the dog. 2 **7** Once you've got help, grab the dog's hind legs. 5

Unit 8 Issues
Lesson 8.1
Listening
1a 2
1b 1 F **2** F **3** T **4** T **5** F
1c driving: pedal, steering wheel, backseat driver, swerve
technology: gadget, gizmo, hand-held device, censor
the voice: unintelligible, husky, squeaky, baritone

Vocabulary
2 1 harm **2** disastrous **3** force **4** indispensable **5** lifesaver **6** overrated **7** waste **8** do **9** benefits **10** underrated

Grammar: reporting verbs
3 1 B and C **2** B and C **3** A and C **4** A and B **5** B and C **6** B

4 1 Mr Blythe reminded us to read the safety precautions. **2** Lena suggested calling a doctor. **3** We had assumed that you knew each other. **4** She accused Tom of stealing the apple. **5** We had to admit that we didn't know the answer. **6** I congratulated her on passing her exam. **7** Dad threatened to stop our pocket money if we continued to behave badly. **8** Clarence denied (ever) meeting her before.

How to: stall for time
5 1 That's a good question. **2** Well, I loved all of them. **3** Let me see. **4** I'd have to think about. **5** That's tricky. **6** That's a difficult question.

91

Lesson 8.2
Grammar: continuous and simple
1 1 h 2 b 3 j 4 g 5 a 6 f 7 i 8 c 9 e 10 d
2 1 had never been 2 had been having 3 was struggling
4 sensed 5 returning 6 had been battling 7 is starting
8 hated 9 put off 10 have been following

Vocabulary: lifestyles
3 1 out 2 buzz 3 crashed 4 hair 5 security 6 and

Reading
4b 1 burst 2 pamper 3 soothing 4 high
5 bottle (something) up 6 sedentary 7 cultivate 8 clutter
4c 1 sedentary 2 soothing 3 bottle up 4 clutter
5 pampers 6 cultivating 7 high 8 burst

Lesson 8.3
Listening
1a and b 1 Chris, Can't come at 6.00. Problem with air conditioning. Will come as soon as possible. 2 Sandy, Small World Travel, Problem with tickets to Fiji. Call 0207 933 6399 3 Partner, Call Dominique about babysitting from 7–12. 4 Alexandra Duvall, customer number 675637, Problem with Classic Body Toner Home Gym. Doesn't work. Send engineer. 5 Liz Jordan, Keynote speaker ill, can't come to conference. Need replacement. Tell William. Call back on the mobile any time.

Grammar: fronting
2 1 thing 2 of the matter 3 point 4 thing you could
5 What irritates 6 What we need 7 remains that
8 What you could try

Vocabulary: cause and effect
3 1 major source 2 far-reaching 3 breeds 4 result
5 had its origins 6 resulted in 7 has its roots 8 leads to
9 bring about 10 consequences

How to: describe everyday problems
4 1 I'm having problems **switching** on the oven. 2 I can't **get** the washing machine to wash the clothes. 3 The computer doesn't **seem** to be working. 4 The car still **won't** start. 5 The clock is always **showing** the wrong time. 6 This light **appears** to be broken. It doesn't switch on.

5a and b 1 <u>The first cause</u> we discovered was a lack of concentration. 4 <u>Consequently</u>, putting it off just adds to that feeling of anxiety, <u>because</u> time is running out. 6 <u>For example</u>, some perfectionists believe they must do extensive research <u>before</u> writing anything. 2 <u>Instead of</u> dealing with the task at hand, many people let their mind wander, staring out of the window or surfing the net. 7 <u>This means that</u> they read and read <u>but</u> never actually get round to writing the paper. 5 <u>A third cause</u> is perfectionism. 3 <u>The second cause</u> was fear; <u>when</u> we are worried that a task is beyond us, we tend to put it off.

Review and consolidation unit 8

Reporting verbs
1 1 June warned them not to go into the house. 2 June claimed the house was haunted. 3 June threatened to tell her mother. 4 Mike accused June of lying. 5 Mike informed Sally that ghosts don't exist. 6 Mike persuaded Sally to go in. 7 Sally agreed to go into the house. 8 June reminded them about (what had happened to) the dog. 9 Mike thanked June for the warning. 10 Later they regretted going into/entering the house.

Vocabulary
2 1 A 2 B 3 A 4 C 5 C 6 B

Continuous aspect
3 1 1 B 2 A 2 1 A 2 B 3 1 A 2 B 4 1 B 2 A 5 1 B 2 A
6 1 A 2 B

Fronting
4 1 The thing that irritates me is all that noise. 2 What worries me is the cost involved. 3 The fact of the matter is I'm tired of this game. 4 What might work is if we open the shop on Sundays. 5 The trouble is there are too many people.
6 The fact remains that he broke his promise. 7 What we needed to have done is eat earlier. 8 The point is the house is in good condition.

Vocabulary
5 1 This toaster keeps **burning** the toast. 2 Let me see.
3 I'd have to think **about** that. I'm pretty busy myself. 4 That's a **tricky** question. 5 My car **won't** start. What can I do? 6 This drawer seems **to be stuck**. How does it open?

6 1 own 2 and 3 – 4 – 5 but 6 by 7 so 8 –
9 a 10 us

7

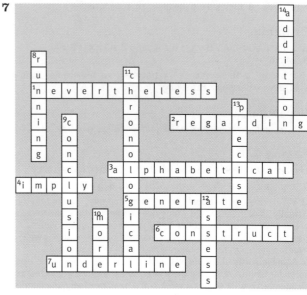

Unit 9 Vision

Lesson 9.1
Vocabulary
1

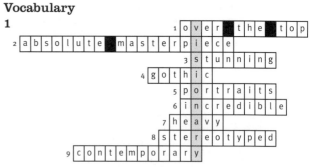

Key word: visionary

Grammar: dependent prepositions
2 1 for 2 of 3 On 4 for 5 from 6 with 7 in 8 for 9 in
10 under 11 from 12 to **Artist:** Van Gogh

How to: express certainty and uncertainty
3 Suggested answers: 1 There is no doubt that he was one of the greatest musicians of all time. 2 We are not 100 percent certain where he was born. 3 The theory was undeniably wrong. 4 The premises on which he based his theories are questionable./He based his theories on questionable premises. 5 It is irrefutable that the damage was caused by the car in question. 6 It is not clear-cut which driver is responsible for the accident. 7 It is debatable but eating small amounts of chocolate may have beneficial health properties. 8 It is indisputable that smoking tobacco limits your life expectancy.

Reading
4a 1 B 2 C 3 B
4b 1 revered 2 pre-eminent 3 groundbreaking 4 grave 5 musings 6 relishes 7 there's no telling 8 assured
4c 1 Hawking was born in Oxford, not London. 2 He studied Physics, not Mathematics. 3 The disease left him severely disabled, but still able to have children. 4 He had financial worries, as his academic salary was not enough to support his full-time medical care. 5 His book was not academic, but a popular science book.

Lesson 9.2
Vocabulary: describing art
1 1 abstract 2 striking 3 avant-garde 4 plain 5 tranquil 6 colourful 7 disturbing 8 stunning 9 traditional 10 dull

How to: say what you like/dislike in general
2 1 I'm afraid it's just not my **kind** of thing at all. 2 It's really not **my** taste. 3 Yes. I'm really **into** her work. 4 It's not really my **cup** of tea. 5 I'm not a big **fan** of his stuff. 6 Brilliant. It's one of my **all-time** favourites. 7 She deserved to. I've always **admired** her work. 8 I just can't **relate** to this kind of thing.

Grammar: discourse markers
3 1 There's been some kind of misunderstanding. 2 I can sort of see what you mean. 3 To be honest, I haven't really understood a word you are talking about. 4 To tell you the truth, I would rather stay at home and watch a film. 5 We can more or less be sure of their intention to purchase. 6 At any rate, we should be able to get a good price. 7 Mind you, I wouldn't want to stay there on my own. 8 As a matter of fact, I think the ideas should be discussed at a meeting. 9 As far as I'm concerned, it is the best offer we are going to get. 10 As for when we should leave, I don't think it makes any difference. 11 As a matter of fact, they proved us wrong in the end. 12 As regards changing the policy completely, I'm not in a position to answer.

Vocabulary: crime
4 1 mastermind 2 hideout 3 undercover 4 tracked 5 stuffed 6 chainsaw 7 crack 8 haul

Reading
5a Momentarily Fooled
5b 1 F 2 F 3 F 4 T 5 T 6 T 7 T 8 F
5c 1 rich and successful 2 amount of something kept in a secret place 3 said to be true 4 to make you worried 5 beautifully, cleverly 6 documents, paintings or money which have been copied illegally 7 tricked 8 escape or avoid

Lesson 9.3
Vocabulary
1 1 holiday snaps 2 foreground 3 out of focus 4 digital 5 disposable 6 accessories 7 flash 8 close-up

Grammar: unreal past
2 1 j 2 h 3 i 4 d 5 a 6 f 7 g 8 b 9 c 10 e
3 1 If only Rashid hadn't lost his passport. 2 It's high time you stopped acting like a child. 3 I would sooner have taken the train. 4 It's about time we got back to work. 5 If you were offered that job, would you accept? 6 Supposing I were to press this button, what would happen? 7 Phyllis wishes she had a baby sister/Phyllis wishes she wasn't an only child. 8 Would you have rather gone out or watched a DVD last night?

How to: respond to hypothetical questions
4 1 It's highly likely I'd agree. 2 I would definitely consider taking them to court. 3 It's unlikely that I'd be able to do that. 4 There's no way that I would do that. 5 I would probably agree to that. 6 I suppose I might consider doing that.

Listening
5a 1 She started by taking photos of her grandmother's garden with a camera which her father gave her. 2 The fact that you didn't have to send the film to be developed, the photo came instantly out of the bottom of the camera. 3 She is interested in lots of different things, and also she doesn't want to be 'pigeonholed' into doing just one type of photography. 4 She's taking pictures of the river at different stages of the day. 5 Water 'has its own sort of visual vocabulary'. Perhaps she means that water has a language of its own. Its message changes all the time, according to how the river looks.
5b Sandrine started by taking photos of tropical flowers in her grandmother's garden at the age of ten. She now photographs many things, including nature and famous people. She thinks a photographer's job is to capture truth and beauty. She says she is interested in everything. Sandrine lives near a river and loves the light there.
5c 1 c 2 h 3 f 4 b 5 g 6 a 7 d 8 e

Review and consolidation unit 9
Dependent prepositions
1a 1 to 2 of 3 in 4 from 5 in 6 in 7 under 8 in 9 on 10 of 11 from 12 of
1b Hi Arline,
How are you? Everything's fine here at Los Alamos. You wouldn't believe some of the scientists I'm working with. There's Hans Vogel, who *specialises in* particle theory. He has really *devoted his life to* his research. He's probably one of the greatest scientists *of all time*. There's also Bernheimer, who won the Nobel Prize *in recognition of* his contribution to our understanding of nanotechnology. He's the world's greatest expert *in the field*. He is totally *immersed in* his work, which is *the development of* a new type of weapon. I've managed to speak to him *on several occasions*, and even though he's working *under pressure*, he doesn't seem to *suffer from* stress.
I've been able to *draw inspiration from* these people and I really hope I can *succeed in* my work here.
Love,
Richard

Discourse markers
2 1 As **a** matter of fact, we found it rather boring. 2 **To** be honest, I don't like ballet much.; As far as the skill is concerned I think it's wonderful, but I can't say I've seen much of it. 3 To tell you **the** truth I think it's a bit overrated. 4 That film was kind **of** long, wasn't it? 5 Bye, Tom! Anyway, Mary, **as I** was saying, that restaurant is fantastic.; Mind **you**, it's not exactly cheap. 6 **At** any rate, I'll get at least two, OK? 7 Frankly, he more **or** less did everything! 8 **What** I was going to say was that I enjoyed the exhibition very much.

Unreal past: *I wish/If only*
3 1 had 2 had poured 3 What if 4 Supposing 5 had been 6 would sooner 7 would rather 8 high time

Vocabulary
4 1 figurative 2 abstract 3 traditional 4 avant-garde 5 stunning 6 disturbing 7 striking 8 tranquil 9 monochrome 10 colourful

5 1 We were able to test a number of patients, but we couldn't prove that the theory was correct. 2 After giving me this wonderful opportunity to teach on a university course, he told me there was a possibility that the course would be cancelled due to lack of numbers. 3 There's a vacancy in that company because one of the employees is on vacation. 4 Baggy trousers don't really suit me, but I can't fit into those tight ones. 5 All those who attended the seminar will be asked to assist at the conference. 6 I'm not doing anything at the moment but tomorrow I'm leaving. No, not tomorrow, on Monday actually. 7 We had a school reunion and I socialised with people I hadn't seen for twenty years! After that we had a meeting to discuss how we could help the school financially.
2 It seemed proper and sensible to make rules related to sensitive issues such as racism and sexism.

6 1 ~~my liking.~~ 2 ~~without a doubt~~ 3 ~~would consider to do that~~ 4 ~~unquestionably~~ 5 ~~without a doubt~~ 6 ~~a big favourite~~ 7 ~~I wouldn't probably do that~~ 8 ~~couldn't agree to them.~~

Unit 10 Feelings

Lesson 10.1
Listening and Vocabulary
1 Suggested answers:
Speaker 1: He's a bit down in the dumps because he isn't enjoying his job or doing the things he wants with his life.
Speaker 2: She's at her wits end with worry because her daughter hasn't been in contact with her.
Speaker 3: She's over the moon about having a baby boy.
Speaker 4: He's really wound up about not being able to get an appointment at the hospital.
Speaker 5: She's in two minds about whether to visit her friends/family.

2 **1** Speaker 3 **2** Speaker 4 **3** Speaker 3 **4** Speaker 4
5 Speaker 5 **6** Speaker 1 **7** Speaker 2 **8** Speaker 2
9 Speaker 1 **10** Speaker 3

Grammar: modals
3 **1** We didn't really need to bring all this equipment. **2** They are bound to find out sooner or later. **3** I think we ought to look around the house first. **4** She is likely to do well in the marathon. **5** There must be an easier way to do this. **6** I've asked her a hundred times already but she won't change her position. **7** They can't charge that much for a service. It's ridiculous. **8** We might bump into you at the party on Saturday. **9** You are supposed to take your shoes off before you go in. **10** It will take a few months before we can move to the new premises.

4 **1** C **2** A **3** B **4** B **5** A **6** C

Vocabulary
5 **1** getting the things we really want out of life **2** tendency
3 dwell **4** look on the bright side **5** chances of success in life seemed slim **6** boost your intuition **7** gut feelings and hunches **8** open to new experiences
9 work out well in the long run

Lesson 10.2
Grammar: modals of deduction
4 **1** It can't have been Pete who you saw. **2** There is no answer. They could have gone to bed. **3** You weren't looking where you were going. The car might have killed you. **4** I'm not sure that they're still in the city. I think they may have moved. **5** I'm glad you came. I couldn't have done it without you. **6** I can't find it anywhere, but it must be here. **7** Rick and June might come to the wedding reception. **8** Someone called and left a message. It may have been Kate. **9** You must be joking. **10** They are still not here. They might have got lost.

Vocabulary: strong adjectives of feeling
2 **1** thrilled **2** furious **3** taken aback **4** ecstatic **5** indifferent
6 miserable **7** chuffed **8** uninterested **9** terrified
10 flabbergasted **11** dumbstruck **12** outraged **13** delighted
14 livid **15** petrified **16** upset

Reading
3a frustration ✓ contentment ✓ fear ✓ regret ✓ surprise ✓ jealousy ✓

3b **frustration:** After 60 years spent suffocating in the upper classes, she did a ...

contentment: For the first time in her life she was happy.

fear: It was sheer terror.

regret: Do you regret it now? 'Yes,' she says, surprising herself.

surprise: 'I think Oprah expected me to cry or something,' she snorts. 'She asked me if I wanted a hug. I said, 'Get away from me, you loon. I'm English'.'

jealousy: he moved a younger woman ('Not that much younger,' sniffs Moon) into the couple's Berkshire village. When he failed to turn up to see his wife one day, she calmly snipped the sleeves off thirty-two of his Savile Row suits, trashed his BMW with a can of white paint and deposited rare wines from his cellar on doorsteps around the village like a milkman.

4 **1** F **2** F **3** F **4** T **5** T **6** T **7** T **8** F

5 **1** spurned spouses **2** wellies **3** jackdaw **4** brisk **5** booms
6 chesterfield **7** crumbled **8** snipped **9** trashed **10** quip
11 getting even **12** dreary

Lesson 10.3
Reading
1 **1** The boys were watching a seagull eating crusts of bread.
2 The builders were in their shed laughing at the seagull when they threw a piece of bread at it and hit its head. **3** The young boys would write their names in the wet cement. **4** The building site moved as they completed the new road. **5** The boys wrote their names in the cement at night when everyone except the watchmen had gone home. **6** The boys only wrote their Christian names in case the builders went around Barrytown from knocking at the doors to find out who had written their names in the cement. **7** They wrote Liam's name and address in black marker pen, on a plastered wall in a new house. **8** The boy's mother looked at his dirty hands and fingernails, and was able to smell the smoke.

Grammar: uses of would
2 **1** The boys would light fires and play on building sites.
2 The builders would find names written in cement in the morning. **3** The boys would only write their Christian names so that the builders wouldn't realise who they were. **4** The men would throw their bread at the seagulls. **5** We would have written all our names on the walls if we'd been brave enough. **6** She told me that we would get into trouble if we went out at night. **7** Would you come over here and show me your hands, Patrick? **8** I wish she wouldn't always tell my dad when I've been naughty.

3 **1** He had always said that he would give me money. (Or He has always said that he will give me money.) **2** The teacher would never smile at me. (Or The teacher wouldn't ever smile at me.)
3 Would you like to follow me to my office? **4** The family moved to the countryside so that they would have a better quality of life.
5 She warned us that the job would be hard. **6** I'd have changed jobs earlier if I had realised how easy it was. **7** No matter how hard they tried, the horse wouldn't leave the stable. **8** Would you turn the lights off when you have finished?

How to: describe a childhood memory
4 **1** sticks **2** always **3** occasion **4** never **5** remember
6 just **7** hardly **8** However **9** felt **10** back

Listening
5 **1** Taking exams when she was younger. **2** No. As a child she enjoyed them, but as she got older she would feel stressed.
3 She would learn the information word for word, like the lines in a play. **4** She needed to apply theory to formulate answers, rather than just rely on the information she had memorised.

6 **1** a bit of a geek – d **2** word for word – a **3** later in life – g
4 you can't really get away with – b **5** learning things by lines – f
6 stressed out – c **7** learnt the lesson – e

Review and consolidation unit 10

Vocabulary
1 **1** I'm in two minds as to whether or not to go to the concert. **2** They are over the moon about becoming grandparents. **3** He's been a bit down in the dumps recently. **4** She was at her wits end about failing the exam.
5 Try not to get so wound up about life. Take it easy. **6** I'm feeling particularly pleased with myself for passing my driving test.
7 The kids have been out all day and they are buzzing with energy.
8 Now all the tickets are sold out so we're kicking ourselves.

Grammar: modals
2 **1** b **2** c **3** a **4** a **5** c **6** c **7** a **8** b **9** b **10** c

Vocabulary
3 **1** At the beginning of the race, his chances of **success** seemed slim. **2** He has a tendency to **dwell** on the negative. **3** I'm sure it will all work **out** well in the long run. **4** Try looking on the **bright** side. **5** Generally, I would say I'm open to new **experiences**. **6** There are various techniques you can use to **boost** your intuition. **7** I try to make sure I'm getting the things I really **want** out of life. **8** My **gut** feeling is that things are going to be fine when we get there.

Vocabulary: strong adjectives of feeling
4 **1** delighted **2** furious **3** taken aback **4** thrilled
5 indifferent **6** miserable **7** uninterested **8** terrified
9 livid **10** upset

Grammar: uses of would

5 When I was younger, my parents were always busy as they had just started their own business, so they often had to go abroad to Thailand and couldn't look after my brother and me. When they went away on these trips, they **would** send us to stay with my grandfather, a fruit farmer who lives at the foot of the mountains. I was always happy when my mother told us we **would** stay with Grandpa, as the time we spent at his house was always a wonderful time. The air there is fresh and clean, and the scenery is beautiful. There is no pollution. In the morning I **would** wake and smell the grass and the flowers, and hear the birds singing their song. There is an orchard filled with fruit trees of many kinds, and we were always happy when our grandfather **would** ask: Would you like to help pick the fruit? When the fruit was ripe, we could pick as much as we could eat. And when there was too much, we **would** set up a street stall, and make good money selling the sweet fruit to passers-by. My grandfather kept dogs and chickens, and took us for walks in the forest towards the mountain. Here he taught us the names of the plants, so that we **would** know which were good to eat, which were useful for medicinal purposes, and which were toxic. He **wouldn't** let us pick the plants until we could tell him what each one was. We learned so much when we were with him, more than we **would** have learned by going to school. I **would** have stayed there forever if it were possible.

Vocabulary: particles

6 **1** under **2** out **3** down **4** up **5** off **6** up **7** around **8** on **9** down **10** out

Pearson Education Limited
Edinburgh Gate
Harlow
Essex CM20 2JE
England
and Associated Companies throughout the world.

www.longman.com

© Pearson Education Limited 2007

The right of Antonia Clare and JJ Wilson to be identified as authors of this Work has been asserted by them in accordance with the Copyright, Designs and Patents Act 1988.

All rights reserved; no part of this publication may be reproduced, stored in a retrieval system, or transmitted in any form or by any means, electronic, mechanical, photocopying, recording, or otherwise without the prior written permission of the Publishers.

First published 2007
Fifth Impression 2010

ISBN 978-0-582-84176-5 (Workbook only without key)
ISBN 978-1-4058-2241-1 (Workbook only with key)
ISBN 978-1-4058-2259-6 (Workbook with key and CD-ROM pack)

Set in 10.5/13pt Meta Plus Book and 10/13pt Meta Plus Normal
Printed in Malaysia (CTP-VVP)

We are grateful to the following for permission to reproduce copyright material:
The Daily Telegraph for 'Feeling on top of the world – with no legs and laryngitis' by Paul Chapman published in *The Daily Telegraph*, 17 May 2006, *The Guardian* for 'Day 15 996: bike stolen in Portsmouth. Day 16,000: nice ride with newspaper chap' by Matt Seaton published in the *The Guardian* May 13, 2006 © Guardian News and Media Limited 2006,Courtney Reid-Eaton for 'Child of the Incarcerated' from American Public Media © Courtney Reid-Eaton; *National Post* for 'Growing ranks of the suddenly rich afflicted with illness', material granted with the express permission of: "National Post Company", a CanWest Partnership, Sheridan Winn for 'Words to the Wise' from *Business Life Magazine* Sept 2005 © Sheridan Winn; *BBC Focus Magazine* for Profile Stephen Hawking. 'How Stephen Hawking beat motor neurone disease and discovered how time began' by Graham Southom Focus, February 2004; John Sutton for 'Paddy Clarke Ha Ha Ha' by Roddy Doyle

In some instances we have been unable to trace the owners of copyright material and we would appreciate any information that would enable us to do so.

Acknowledgements
The publishers and author(s) would like to thank the following people and institutions for their feedback and comments during the development of the material:
Fiona Gallagher, Republic of Ireland; Elizabeth Gregson, Italy; Sarah Gumbrell, England

Illustrated by: Roger Penwill, Brian Lee and Lucy Truman (New Division)

Cover design by Zeke Design

Photo Acknowledgements
We are grateful to the following for permission to reproduce photographs:
(Key: b-bottom; c-centre; l-left; r-right; t-top)
4 Getty Images: Simon Fergusson. **6 Ardea:** John Daniels (c). **Popperfoto.com:** (t). **Wikipedia:** University of California Museum of Anthropology (b). **12 Alamy Images:** (tr); Liyako Matsuda (cl). **16 Alamy Images:** Peter Horree (c); Alain Machet (tr). **Art Directors and TRIP photo Library:** Spencer Grant (tl). **28 Ronald Grant Archive:** Columbia Pictures Corporation and Marvel Enterprises (bl). **Kobal Collection Ltd:** Universal / Marvel Entertainment (c); Warner Bros / DC Comics (tr). **32 Getty Images:** Ami Vitale. **46 Alamy Images:** Imagestate. **52 EMPICS:** South Yorkshire Police. **54 Alamy Images:** David Lyons (tr). **Corbis:** (tl). **Rex Features:** The Travel Library (bl). **71 Getty Images:** Time Life Pictures. **83 Rex Features:** Image Source

All other images © Pearson Education

Cover images by Superstock (t), Alamy (l) (Nagelstock.com), Punchstock (b) (Digital Vision).

Picture research by Kevin Brown

Every effort has been made to trace the copyright holders and we apologise in advance for any unintentional omissions. We would be pleased to insert the appropriate acknowledgement in any subsequent edition of this publication.